What was the Vietnam War like for American volunteer doctors who served there? For the author of this book, it was an attempt to work in a medical program designed to win the Vietnamese people away from the Vietcong.

However, Dr. Byerly also found that the Vietnam War meant wearing a sweat-drenched shirt plastered to one's back, being lost in the confusion of broken syllables that constitute another man's language, coping with the surrealistic situation of the staff insistence on neglecting a bleeding young woman and leaving her lying on a table because it was siesta time, a lack of penicillin caused by its being held back in the storeroom for emergencies, finding oneself suddenly doing emergency work on a Vietcong patient under the silent surveillance of his intently watching compatriots. War meant having to suffer with the patient, knowing that the type of one-to-one medicine practiced could never match the benefits of a public health program and proper sanitation.

Here is the war made vivid in a moving account of the carnage and horror in a Vietnamese provincial hospital, a keenly dramatic, searing, true-life account that is as explosive and contemporary as today's headlines.

NAM DOC

NAM DOC

by
Wesley Grimes Byerly, Jr.

VANTAGE PRESS
New York / Washington / Atlanta
Los Angeles / Chicago

Published by Vantage Press, Inc.
516 West 34th Street, New York, New York 10001

Manufactured in the United States of America
ISBN: 0-533-04499-5

Library of Congress Catalog Card No.: 79-56098

CONTENTS

LIST OF
MAPS AND ILLUSTRATIONS

From the *Saigon POST*
January 10, 1964
Saigon, Republic of South Vietnam

"TO RALLY THE PEASANTS"

The main obstacle barring the government from reaching the peasants' hearts stems from the peasants' innate mistrust of officials. This mistrust, accumulated through decades of colonist rule, has been compounded even more by the misrule and mishandling of Diem's lieutenants.

Peasant grievances against local officials of the Ngo Dinh Diem government have become almost endemic. Most of these grievances were justified. Cases of extortion, bribery, intimidation, arbitrary arrest, summary execution and mass torture were commonplace.

In many instances, peasant grievances are the result of tactical errors committed by well-meaning commanders. Cases have been reported of wanton bombing or shelling of entire villages where, it was later learned, only a handful of VC had been detected. Sometimes these grievances are explained away as the consequences of war. The merciless destruction of unharvested ricefields under a column of armored personnel carriers, or the scorched earth of napalm bombing are examples of this type of grievance.

Yet all these indirect causes are forgivable. What cannot be forgiven is the sad but commonplace case of abuse by district chiefs—more often, by their deputy chiefs—for security. Name a single delta province where the deputy's name is not whispered with fear among the peasant population, and with a furtive, over-the-shoulder glance.

In the days of the late Ngo Dinh Diem, the deputy chief for security's name was synonymous with affluence, quick money, and several wives. And no one dared complain. Under Diem, an accusation against a district chief, province chief, or their deputy was tantamount to subversive propaganda.

Since the Revolution, a massive overhaul of personnel has been effected, down to the district level. Yet, is there any assurance that the same mistakes as those which drove millions of peasants into the arms of the Vietcong will not be repeated? What are a peasant's chances against an abusive official, under the new government?

On the answers of these questions depend whether the peasant will look to the government for protection of his person, his rights, and his property, or to the Vietcong. And we must not forget that as long as there is one aggrieved peasant, there are ten potential Vietcong sympathizers, and as many potential recruits. And every new case of abuse will widen the gap between this essential war factor and the government.

Quoted from: *The Viet-Nam Reader.*
Edited by Marcus G. Raskin and Bernard B. Fall.
New York: Vintage Books of Random House, 1967.

INTRODUCTION

In 1952, the health effort of the United States Agency for International Development began in Indochina, which then comprised Cambodia, Laos, Tonkin, Annam, and Cochin China (the three latter countries forming North and South Vietnam). The effort was small and developmental. After French Indochina was dissolved and the two Vietnams established in 1954, a small USAID section continued in South Vietnam. The emphasis was on public health, education, and malaria control.

In 1954, the Geneva Convention set the stage for the division of Indochina. Based on the anticipations of: (1) the French, (2) the Vietnamese (all areas), (3) other Indochinese, (4) the Americans, and (5) the rest of the world, the settlement, as it finally evolved, meant different things to the different groups. The Southeast Asian Treaty Organization (SEATO) later in 1954 gave an identity to South Vietnam, and the U.S. committed itself to building a pro-American state based on our philosophy of "falling dominos," current at that time. Each president accepted this policy, and each expanded upon it in his turn: Eisenhower, Kennedy, and Johnson, so that by the end of 1963, more than 16,500 U.S. military personnel were involved and 500 casualties had resulted.

In October 1955, Diem proclaimed himself president of the Republic of South Vietnam. From here on, the United States got progressively into deeper trouble in Vietnam.

The U.S. put its emphasis upon teaching "democracy," to help South Vietnam achieve a democratic revolution, and upon giving increasing economic and military assistance. The North Vietnamese, meanwhile, were themselves committed to a political rather than a military strategy during this time.

In 1955, the United States Operations Mission became the local branch of the Department of State Agency for International Development. USOM had three major efforts: (1) commercial import, (2) technical assistance, and (3) counterinsurgency. The divisions of these programs, to mention a few, ranged from agriculture, fishing, and education through public administration, to police, public works, and public health, etc.

In these years, from the mid-fifties (1954) to the early sixties (1960–1961), there was relative peace in South Vietnam. Between 1960 and 1962, Vietcong terrorism progressed to the point that, by 1962, the VC were making 100 attacks per week in some parts of South Vietnam, ranging in attacks from squad to battalion size, and some 25,000 Vietnamese were killed. During these years, the author Bernard Falls made his studies and trips in and out of Vietnam, noting the increasing size of revolutionary activity.

In 1962, the National Security Council recommended that the American civil-assistance agencies take a more active part in the counterinsurgency program and, in that year, the first USAID direct-assistance medical element was established in the form of a surgical team.

In 1962–63, convinced that Vietnamese civilian care would need more assistance beyond what the Vietnamese were able to do, the president of South Vietnam asked President Kennedy for American assistance. At this time, nearly all of South Vietnam's doctors were in the military or were leaving the country for France, and the refugee problem was increasing in the South. The problem was handed to the State Department, hence, to USAID and USOM.

In 1963 and 1964, the USAID Health Program in Vietnam had been directed toward two major components: (1) medical-dental education and (2) health development, which included rural health, malaria eradication, nursing-health activities, and limited clinical-medical support in the form of surgical teams. The emphasis was upon rural health and public health at the village and hamlet level.

By the end of 1963, the United States (for whatever reason, being grossly misled) was very optimistic about progress in South Vietnam, about the effectiveness of American aid, and the success of the Strategic Hamlet program.

With the assassination of Diem on 1 November 1963, the American and South Vietnamese positions deteriorated drastically. From then until the summer of 1965, seven military dictatorships came and went. This demonstrated three facts: (1) Anyone who ruled the country needed U.S. support. (2) Even with U.S. support, anyone who ruled had to accommodate the Buddhists. (3) Anyone whom the U.S. backed, because they were not neutral, lacked the support of large segments of the population.

In 1963, Dr. Malcolm Phelps visited an old flying friend, Major General Rollin Anthis, United States Air Force, in Vietnam where the general was in charge of the air force counterinsurgency program. During the course of this visit and later in Washington, D.C., General Anthis told Dr. Phelps that he felt that a medical program directed toward the civilian population would go a long way toward winning the Vietnamese people away from the Vietcong and to the side of the government.

Dr. Phelps became interested and, after several meetings with members of the State Department's Agency for International Development (USAID), the groundwork was laid for a program that would send American volunteer physicians to Vietnam on a short-term basis to give civilian medical care.

CIVILIAN MEDICAL FACILITIES

In 1965, the estimated population of South Vietnam was 15,500,000, increasing at 300,000 to 400,000 a year. No national census had been taken, but it was estimated that there were about 900 "Western-type" physicians in South Vietnam, giving a physician-to-patient ratio of one to 17,200. However, 650 of the country's physicians were in the military service to care for a half million in the armed forces and their two million dependents. This left the remaining 250 to care for 13,000,000 people—obviously, an impossible task!

There were approximately sixty hospitals, varying in size from 35 to 1,500 beds, almost all built in the late 1800s and early 1900s. Ninety percent had no running water, no waste disposal, and little or no power facilities. Rural health facilities consisted of 163 maternity-infirmary-dispensary buildings (MID's) for 236 districts. Twenty-five thousand villages were each supposed to have a maternity-dispensary, but only 342 were in existence. Six thousand hamlets (smaller than villages) were supposed to have health stations, but did not. Medical equipment was outdated French or cast-off modern donations from many different countries—a maintenance nightmare. "The medical supply situation was atrocious—no supply catalogs, no standard items, no stock control—entire operation based on guesswork. Supply distribution was abysmal. All stocks were located in Saigon." (Ref. 1)

The Vietnamese ministry of health had no goals, no short- or long-term plans, except in malaria and tuberculosis control and maternal-child health.

About 85 percent of the 7,000 rural health workers had not been paid. With inflation rampant, the cost of living going up, increased draft quotas to the military, the danger of living and working in the rural areas; all these contributed to a situation in which the trained rural work force was rapidly depleted.

To assist the hospitals at the provincial level, the United States instituted a Military Provincial Hospital Assistance Program (MILPHAP). This consisted of teams composed of three medical officers, an administrator, and twelve enlisted men. One team was assigned to each hospital. The U.S. Army Surgeon General's office managed the MILPHAP program, but drew personnel from the U.S. Army, Navy, and Air Force. In Vietnam, the teams were under USOM (USAID) control. The American armed forces conducted their own program to improve the health of Vietnamese civilians through their own Medical Civic Action Program (MEDCAP).

Also, the medical effort from "third countries" (such as Australia, New Zealand, Iran, Philippines, West Germany) was similarly organized, with medical teams assigned to the various province hospitals as regional hospital teams. All of these teams operated under the overall direction of the USOM health division.

"Project Vietnam" was grafted onto the USOM health-divisions structure. The People-to-People Health Foundation, Inc., was contracted by USAID to administer the "Project Vietnam" program. The American Medical Association would help recruit the doctors.

In August 1965, Doctor Richard E. Perry of St. Petersburg, Florida, arrived in Saigon as the first volunteer physician to serve under the people-to-people program, and "Project Vietnam" was born.

From August 1965 to June 1966, approximately 120 American physicians volunteered to serve for periods of sixty days or more in Vietnam, providing civilian medical care working in the provincial hospitals.

This people-to-people pilot project ended in June 1966. That month the House of Delegates of the AMA sanctioned the undertaking of this program. President Johnson and USAID accepted the American Medical Association's agreement to continue the program.

Dr. Phelps then went to Saigon on July 8, 1966, to head the AMA operation in Vietnam. He was to be liaison field director between the AMA, the physicians, USAID, and the Ministry of Health of the Republic of Vietnam.

Under the aegis of the AMA, "Project Vietnam" became the "Volunteer Physicians for Vietnam" (VPVN). Under this program, the doctors volunteered for a two-month tour of work in the province hospitals and received travel expenses plus ten dollars per day for living expenses. USAID financed the program.

The volunteers worked with teams of U.S. military physicians or with volunteer surgical teams from other nations. These teams were assigned to USAID and served for one year in provincial civilian hospitals to provide continuity to the U.S. medical-assistance programs. The volunteer physicians provided additional medical expertise, augmenting the civilian care programs.

The greatest demand was for general and orthopedic surgeons to treat war-related civilian casualties. However, general practitioners, internists, ophthalmologists, pediatricians, and preventive-medicine specialists also served.

Under the AMA-USAID program, thirty-two physicians were sent every two months, with sixteen volunteers rotating home each month. To be accepted as a volunteer, the physician had to be in good health and capable of withstanding the work load, stresses, and rigors of a tropical environment. He had to be vaccinated against smallpox, inoculated against cholera, immunized against plague, typhoid, tetanus, typhus, and poliomyelitis.

NAM DOC

PROLOGUE

The *AMA News* (volume 9 number 23) of June 6, 1966, had as its editorial "Volunteers for Vietnam." The next-to-the-last paragraph read, "This service is in the best tradition of the medical profession. Physicians have traditionally done much to aid the victims of disaster and the effects of the conflict on the civilian population of Vietnam offer another opportunity."

Spurred by this and the knowledge that a friend and physician colleague in Hickory had been there a few months before, I immediately wrote Dr. Edwin W. Brown, Jr., the program director for Project Vietnam. This was described as "a cooperative medical effort of America's inter-voluntary agencies for the People of South Vietnam, with the assistance of the American Medical Association and the Agency for International Development."

Within the week, I had had a reply and was told that forty surgeons had served in the program since 1965. The essence and workings of the program were outlined in a brochure as follows:

PROJECT VIETNAM

Project Vietnam is limited to the recruitment of physicians on a short-term voluntary basis, for a minimum period of 60 days in Vietnam. Exceptions to the 60-day minimum are not possible. It cannot offer long-term employment on a salaried basis, nor is it able to offer voluntary assignments to persons other than physicians with an M.D. degree. At the present time, it is not possible to utilize female physicians in the program due to prevailing conditions in Vietnam. United States citizenship is required. Under present U.S. Government regulations, it is not possible for any dependents to accompany the volunteer, even if the dependent is medically qualified.

The most pressing need continues to be for orthopedic surgeons, for the majority of admissions to the civilian hospitals of Vietnam are of persons sustaining war injuries, with orthopedic problems comprising a large portion of these injuries to the civilian population.

General practitioners and internists can be utilized in relatively large numbers. General surgeons are also needed, and a very limited number of persons in the fields of chest disease, ophthalmology, otolaryngology, radiology, and psychiatry will be required in 1966. At the present time it is not possible to utilize other specialties, although inquiries are invited from persons in these specialties in anticipation of possible future needs.

In every instance, the need is for men in good health, able to withstand the rigors of a tropical climate. Because of the rigorous nature of the voluntary assignment, an age limit of 55 has recently been imposed. The ability to work well with professional colleagues under difficult and often frustrating conditions is a distinct requirement.

The success of the volunteer program in Vietnam has resulted in its rapid expansion, and volunteers are now being assigned to a larger number of provincial hospitals than the four mentioned on page two of the brochure.

The provincial hospital medical program in Vietnam is being expanded through the use of additional military teams, assigned to the Agency for International Development for service in the civilian provincial hospitals. These MILPHAP teams, as they are called, will each comprise three medical officers, one administrative officer, and twelve enlisted men (corpsmen). Their responsibility will be for the civilian population in the province to which they are assigned. Project Vietnam volunteer physicians will work with these teams in the provincial hospitals, as well as with the other United States and free-world medical teams now serving in Vietnam. It is through these teams that continuity is provided to the volunteer program.

I thought about it for a month, then applied. A month later,

I received notice that I had been accepted. In October, I had notification that I would go with a February increment and received detailed instructions on the many things that had to be done.

It was only three and a half months away, and I had to begin arranging my practice coverage, notifying hospital staffs and organizations for leaves of absence, and swapping around and getting coverage for my obligatory hospital services in the emergency and surgery departments. A passport and visas had to be obtained; this meant digging out long-forgotten birth and marriage certificates. Also, early on, I had to begin to take my immunizations, as I would be going into one of the worst disease-ridden areas of the world. I would have to be immunized against smallpox, cholera, plague, typhoid, tetanus, typhus, polio, diphtheria, and yellow fever. Then, just before leaving, I had to take gamma globulin for protection against hepatitis and viral infections and to begin malaria prophylaxis medication. It seemed like every week or so I was being shot, and my arms and hips were constantly sore from sixteen shots between Thanksgiving and Christmas!

Insurance arrangements had to be made, photographs taken, tickets obtained, travel itinerary lined up, and clothing secured. A trial of packing and repacking to get everything within the allotted sixty-six pounds was done. (The standard allowance of forty-four pounds was allowed, plus an additional twenty-two pounds. We were to pay for the excess baggage on our return.) Travelers' checks had to be bought, for we would have no money income while "in country," although we were informed that there wouldn't be very much to purchase anyhow!

CHAPTER ONE

TO THE WHITE CITY

When war blows dustily over the earth
It is women who suffer:
O Heaven, so blue, so high,
Who shall we blame?

Lament for a Warrior's Wife
—Dang Tran Con

What a wonderful way to go to a war: in an air-conditioned jet, full of good food and drink, and with a beautiful woman beside you!

So it was on 23 January 1967 from the airport in Hickory, North Carolina, I left for the beginning of a long trip to Vietnam and around the world. The stewardess had wondered at all the commotion and why the big send-off? My pastor and his wife, old friends: the Mosbys; Peggy and Juanita (arriving late with the rice!); my mother, who would be baby-sitting at home; our children; and other well-wishers all shouted and yelled and laughed. We took movies and pictures and hugged last-minute good-byes and then were off, for the sun was fast sinking on that sunny but cool winter afternoon.

Seventy minutes later, we changed planes in Atlanta where we wrote hurried postcards to the children and boarded our DC-8.

It was a beautifully smooth flight, with a full moon visible out of our window. I noted that perhaps only a third of the passengers on the almost-filled airplane were civilians, and the remainder were all varieties of the military. It reminded one of the train travel in the wartime 1940s. My wife and I were both famished, as it had been a long time since breakfast. After what seemed an unusually excellent airlines meal of shish kebab, we dozed and the four-and-a-half-hour flight passed too quickly. However, flying at 550 miles per hour at 35,000 feet boggles the mind in terms of time and distance. Beginning our descent over the California Sierra Madre Mountains, we made a foggy approach into San Francisco.

Getting our bags and a minibus, we were sent, as prearranged, to the nearby Hilton Inn with an elegant room for a good night's sleep.

The next morning, by a combination of jitneys and buses, we made our way into downtown San Francisco where I renewed my acquaintance and my wife made hers with that fabulous city. We did the shopping bit, the tour thing (I am a great believer in tours for learning as much as possible about a place in the shortest time. Afterward, on one's own, one can savor the place at one's leisure), and we did a great deal of walking.

One day, our walking was not by choice. We had taken the Powell Street cable car over to Fisherman's Wharf and had eaten lunch at Tarantino's. Coming back up Nob Hill, the cable car broke down and we had to get off with the others and walk. It was cool and raining, not hard, but it was an uncomfortable winter drizzle. We walked up and down several hills and, becoming tired, finally found another cable car and rode a while, only to discover we were going in the wrong direction and had to retrace our steps! We saw all of the regular tourist sites and, over the course of three days and nights, poked into all parts of San Francisco. The Chinatown section was of particular fascination to us, in view of my impending Orient excursion.

We were very impressed by San Francisco (never called by the Barbary-Coast name of "Frisco," but always "San Francisco," for it was named in honor of a saint). The air was so clean and clear, without any smoke or soot. This plus many of the buildings gave the entire city a white, light look: The White City by the Bay. In our many travels worldwide, my wife and I categorize the places, tours, nations, people, by some phrase of description that catches the fancy of both. When it strikes us, we know that is how we always remember and think of that particular time and place. Even the old buildings and homes seemed neat, and the streets were clean. Everywhere there were pretty flowers for sale. There seemed to be a general absence of the police and there was a pervading politeness and helpfulness about the people. The drug culture of

Haight-Ashbury was seemingly secluded, and it was more of a "nighttime tourist attraction" than anything else. MacArthur Park was filled with people of all sorts, including friendly hippies. I did not feel the viciousness in the air that I was to detect a few years later.

One night, at that famous American landmark, the "Top of the Mark," I received my introduction to Vietnam.

It began during the course of an evening tour around San Francisco. We noticed a youngish-appearing, nice-looking, darker-skinned man who sat across the tour bus from us and later shared the back seat of the bus. After a couple of stops and a few pleasantries, we were on to the fact he was Mexican and a doctor. This gave me the entree and after some introductions and in the course of several hours of conversations, interrupted by the tour stops, we learned he was a gynecologist from Mexico City. (He presented us with his calling card and, much to my embarrassment, I couldn't reciprocate, never having gone in for that sort of thing.) He was married and had three children: a six-year-old boy, a four-year-old girl, and a two-year-old boy. They were all at home, and Armand was in San Francisco on a lark. At the finish of the tour, we were downtown and it seemed too early to go in, so we decided on the tourist thing and hopped the cable car up Nob Hill and to the Top of the Mark. There Armand was, a Mexican, drinking Irish whiskey (and my wife her inevitable whiskey sours).

By then, he had found out what the purpose of my being there was and proceeded to politely castigate me and America (meaning the U.S., for isn't Mexico American too? and North American at that). Anyhow, he felt rather strongly that we should not be involved in Vietnam, we should have never been messed up, and that we should get out!

During our night's conversing, it was apparent that Armand was well educated and well traveled and knew his classic opera. He spoke excellent English, although he did have trouble with my Southern drawl, which isn't too mushy, and the idioms of my speech. We were continually amused by him, because his speech, actions, and entire demeanor seemed to be very typical of the slow, sleepy, under-the-sombrero-by-the-cactus-si-senor Mexican.

7

Near the end of the evening, he finished with a long polemic about Russia and the Chinese, believing them to be nonthreatening. "You Americans think everything that is not like you is Communist."

In spite of our differences, we parted the greatest of companions, exchanging addresses and promises to write.

Looking out over the beautifully sparkling city in the black night, I was disturbed that someone, a total stranger, had so doubted "my good intentions and beliefs." Still, I slept soundly.

CHAPTER TWO

THE LAST SUPPER

> Fine, fireplace, glow,
> Wine warms in the hand.
> Snow blows through the door,
> Wind sprays hail on the river.
>
> *The Four Seasons—Winter*
> —Ngo Chi Lan

The next day was cloudy and raining. We ate breakfast late; then I went to see if I could find some other volunteer physicians. Our original orders had been to assemble at the Hilton Inn on Thursday evening, the twenty-sixth of January. There we were to meet with Dr. Moseley and have a dinner briefing and get-together. I couldn't find anyone, or anyone who seemed to know what it was all about. After a while, a spectacled, worried-appearing man in leisure clothes introduced himself and said there had been a snowstorm in the Midwest and that Dr. Moseley was snowbound and probably wouldn't get there. So Dr. Chasler (who worried over us like a mother hen) was sort of in charge. I said "Right ho," and my wife and I shoved off for the metropolis. We did some shopping for the children and, of course, finally ended up at Fisherman's Wharf, where we ate steamed clams at streetside under the umbrella and later went into the Grotto, where we sat for a long time by an open fireplace, talking of home and children and times gone by.

8

At seven that evening, we all gathered in Parlor B. Except for the flying hours together and another meal over two months later, we were never ever together again. Yet we were all doing the same thing and sharing in a strange, unbelievable adventure. A group of middle-aged American doctors going into an unexplainable war in an unknown land, among an unfathomable people with an uncertain future, armed only with their medical knowledge and faith in a desire to serve mankind. It was truly unbelievable!

Chas was now the leader by default, as Dr. Moseley had not shown and somehow, by phone contact, the mantle of authority had been passed to him. He was quiet, but worrisome and continued to go over his lists with a frequent "Oh my, they're still not here." He sat crossed-legged on the bed in bright bathing trunks and repeatedly told of having had to leave so hurriedly from Pittsburgh that he still didn't have his passport and had somehow lost his tickets! Nonetheless, Chas made himself the perfect host, getting names correctly, introducing people, seating us correctly, generally organizing everything, and running the show.

The group was heavy with surgeons. We were told that this was probably the single biggest need, because the provincial hospitals had no Vietnamese surgeons, and the war-casualty loads needed surgical care, as opposed to other things.

There was Ernie from Denver; Ed from the University of Iowa: a young-appearing, aggressive, cigar-smoking, medical-school type. D. J. was in the Veterans Administration at Prescott, Arizona. He was going back for his second tour. We were all eager to know why he was going again, and his philosophically rhetorical reply was, "Why are you all going the first time?"

Kimbrough was a quiet, thoughtful, orthopedic surgeon from Columbia, South Carolina. The other general surgeon besides myself was Sam (the Red Baron). Three were general practitioners: John Mc. of South Dakota, Bob S. of Ohio ("The only reason there are so many Southerners in the group is 'Yew All' didn't get the Medicare and therefore have to go to Vietnam to get work"), and Bill Tatem of New Hampshire. The internist, Jack, was a mustachioed, quiet, pipe-smoking Midwesterner from the Department of Medicine at the University of Oklahoma. He had recently returned from Tokyo and was formulating plans to set up a reciprocal, internal-medicine program between the University of Saigon and the University of Oklahoma.

Two ophthalmologists, Professor Bob Reinecke and his senior resident, Reed Roberts, from Harvard's Massachusetts Eye and Ear Infirmary, rounded out the group assembled. Three members of the slated levy were absent, but no one seemed to know exactly who they were or why they weren't present.

The ice of unfamiliarity was easily broken with cocktails and similarity of background: three of us were from Carolina, four of us had been at Harvard, five were medical-school teachers, etc.

We had a delicious, thick, roast-beef meal, and Chas kept referring to it as "the last supper." (Without sacrilege!)

About the only real information we got was that we were to leave in the morning at 9 A.M. on a breakfast flight: Pan American 001. Everyone was enthusiastic. I was impressed that everyone could not give a good reason for going, i.e., at least none would verbalize it.

We finally arrived at a consensus when someone said, "It is a chance to do something for your country and to do something personally for people who wouldn't survive if you were not there."

We couldn't get a whole lot of individual tidbit information out of D.J. He merely said we'd each have different experiences and would have to evaluate them individually.

(I am sure this was true. However, in the years afterward, I read all sorts of stories about Vietnam and was continually amazed how many little things coincided. How many people's opinions about things like the country, the conduct of the war, the people, were more or less also what I experienced.)

Again, we broke up about ten. Some went to the bar for a nightcap; others out on the town.

By midnight, I was all packed, paperwork done, last letters written, early wake-up call left, and to bed.

Vietnam, here we come!

CHAPTER THREE

THE TRIP OVER (AND THE RED BARON)

So I'm sober, so I'm drunk, huh?
So I fool around with the moon in broad daylight?
Sure: if nobody plays in that tiger's den
How would you get a little tiger in your arms?

Three Exchanges with Chieu Ho
—Ho Xuan-Huong

The jangle of the telephone awakened us at a quarter to six. We fixed coffee in the room, dressed, and did final packing. I checked out, and we took the minibus to the airport.

I checked in my baggage and declared my camera. Then we went to the Delta Departure area, and I sent Kay home. I wished for a longer good-bye together. I stood on the top of the observation roof and watched until her plane took off. It had been such a wonderful few days—together longer than we had been, just the two of us, in many years and I hated to see her go. There were some doubts for the first time, the dawning realization of the potentials for harm and disaster. I dismissed them.

My shoes had been so wet from the past few days in the rain that I stopped for the luxury of a real shoeshine. After checking in at Pan Am, I had a solitary breakfast, for which I was not particularly anxious. The loudspeaker assembled us at the departure gate, and we had several pictures taken (none of which, I confess, I ever saw) by total group and by specialty group.

At nine o'clock A.M. Pacific Standard Time, we were airborne on Flight 001, a far cry from the China Clipper of the 1930s. I remember sending off to get a first-day-of-issue cover with a special cachet on the envelope for the first flight way back in 1939! How proud I was of that envelope and how it spurred me to a boyhood, stamp-collecting hobby!

This was my first international-flight experience and one of the few really long flights across the country I'd taken, so I was interested in everything. I was just too fascinated with the headset devices for plugging into the radio channels: seven with one set aside for the TV sets. These sixteen-inch-sized screens spaced every ten feet along the overhead storage racks showed an English movie (Kaleidoscope). I could listen to Brahms in one ear, to my seatmate in the other, write, watch television, and daydream to myself all at the same time! Sort of mind boggling!

My seatmates were Behringer, a senior medical student from Missouri, and Kimbrough, the orthopedic surgeon from Columbia, South Carolina. Behringer had been a B-52 pilot in his military-service days before going to medical school. Riding a 707 was a bit different than jockeying a B-52 over the Pacific, and he worried about every squeak, groan, and bump. We had one short storm with some turbulence for fifteen minutes, and he sweated through that. Otherwise, the weather was really very pretty.

Climbing out from San Francisco, we made a long, sweeping, climbing turn, taking us through scattered cloud layers, then into broken layers, finally out, and then on top. It was a beautiful sight, watching the bay get smaller, the shoreline coming on, the ocean getting larger, and then finally realizing we were in another ocean and another world.

My other seatmate was a Georgia-born, spectacled, quiet father of three small girls. I suspected he was beginning to miss them as much as I was beginning to miss my three little ones and beginning to wonder if this trip was really a very smart idea.

At 550 miles per hour, even into a headwind at 35,000 feet, the five and a half hours to Hawaii seemed to pass very quickly. We had one long cocktail hour, one long meal, and one long line to the toilet!!

We passed over Diamond Head and, descending past Hickam Field, made an easy approach into Honolulu Airport. It was just as I thought it would be. It was noon (12:30 Hawaii time) and beautiful, clear, and quite warm. My wool gray-flannel suit and suede vest were quite out of place here.

There were Hawaiian girls placing leis on everyone and generally much merry-making, laughter, and joking. I took some movies and pictures and wrote some cards to the children.

Three hours later, we were on our way again. After the takeoff, the stewardesses improved on the hot, wet, facecloth custom of refreshing oneself before landing: they passed out cold, wet face-cloths, and this was most pleasant after the hot ground stay. An hour later, the captain announced we were flying over an atoll called Frenchman's Shoals at 31,000 feet, and it would be the last ground contact until Tokyo nine and a half hours later.

Crossing the International Date Line, we flew from Friday into Saturday and hadn't even passed through nighttime. This put many of us trying to decide the times in various places—if it is 4:30 but not in the afternoon and it is 7:30 where we were at 9:30 and what day it is where we are going and so on. It occupied time.

During our stopover in Honolulu, we lost Chas. He had shep-herded and guided us to that point, still worried about the "three no-shows." He still had not gotten his passport and so could go no further. I gathered he planned to wait there and come along later. We all had a message from Dr. Moseley in Chicago, apologizing for not being in San Francisco and wishing us good luck.

After leaving Honolulu, our seating arrangements changed, and I sat next to a young staff sergeant returning to Vietnam after a month home. He was with the 15th Medical Battalion at An Khe, and we talked of the war. The plane was full, practically all civilians, as the stops were to be Tokyo and Hong Kong. I was amazed to think of that many American businesses requiring all these types over there.

During the long air flight, I read two books—*Vietnam Diary* by Richard Tregaskis and *LBJ Brigade* by William Wilson.

It seemed that all we did was drink and eat. The drinks were plentiful, and the meals always comprised two courses with drinking between and afterward. There was a great deal of standing in the aisles and moving around: hours of sitting cramped sort of got to one after a while. With this moving around, we all came to know Sam for the first time.

He had an aisle seat, and when he wasn't drinking he was sleeping. We never saw him move, eat, go to the toilet, or do anything except booze! So by the time we reached Hong Kong, he had quite a few admirers of his ability to hold fluids and guzzle the booze!

We had a rough, foggy, instrument landing into Haneda and arrived about 5:30 in the afternoon (Saturday). Behringer, the B-52 pilot, was shaken with the landing, so I took him into the terminal to the bar and bought him a Sapporo beer. The evening air was cold and it was raining and dark, but felt good. We wandered around, bought some trinkets, wrote cards to the children, and then off again.

We climbed back to 31,000 feet and four and a half hours to Hong Kong. The folding bar reappeared, and we ate again the whole way!

Sam drank and slept. No one could remember whether he even got off in Tokyo or woke up. At 10 P.M. Hong Kong time, we set down at Kai Tak Airport twenty-four and a half hours after leaving San Francisco. It had finally gotten to be nighttime, but on another day.

We proceeded through the immigration, passport, and customs areas. I had to open my suitcase. The hotel had porters and drivers with Rolls-Royce limos lined up, waiting, and they whisked us across town. The Chinese bellboys in white took our bags and led us to separate, spacious, scrumptious, luxurious rooms. The Peninsula Hotel lived up to its reputation.

I spent an hour reading all the booklets, cards, and things, getting myself oriented in the hotel, and undressed and bathed. I'd been without sleep and on the go for thirty-six hours and thought I'd simply pass out.

I was mistaken. I slept fitfully off and on for three hours and woke up at 3 A.M. wide awake and the closest to being really homesick since I was young. I just couldn't shake the desire, the urge, the tremendous need to be with the children and Kay. When you realize you can't just pick up the phone and say "hello" or check up on things and wonder if everything is all right, you get a bit of panic. I had a bad several hours of wild dreams and tried walking around to get the cobwebs out and settle myself down.

In finally gave up, got up, had to use a straight razor with soap to shave, and then, after a cold shower, managed to get myself down to breakfast.

We ate in the lobby area with excellent service, an American

14

breakfast. I had wondered what one would eat in China for breakfast, but fried eggs, ham, toast, juice, and jasmine tea seemed to be it.

At breakfast, several of us teamed up and decided to go out on the town. Ed had the name of a Chinese couple from a friend of his. He called them, and they offered to take us into town and show us around. I gathered that the whole process was quite common and usual and although one might think we were being "taken," I could see nothing wrong with the whole business as I looked back on it later.

We were joined by Sam, who seemed to have finally come alive, and we were pleased by his appearance. During the course of the day, his sarcastic, Southern mountain witticisms and comments kept us in stitches. About eight o'clock, a young middle-aged Chinese couple, Julia Wong and Michael Lee, appeared with their English Ford car. They were to drive us on a special sight-seeing tour of Hong Kong, including visits to stores to buy things as well. It seems that she owned a sweater shop, and he owned a tailoring shop.

Although it was Sunday and although they were Roman Catholic, it didn't seem to be a typical American religious day. We learned this was a holiday time, and streets and shops were full. No one goes to church (among the Christians), and most of the millions are Buddhist anyhow. The weather was fair, overcast, and warm.

We were taken first to the tailoring shop where the work on our tailor-made suits was begun. This was my introduction into the Hong Kong suit, and it was fascinating. I opted for summer suits, figuring I'd get more wear out of that by the time I got home. Within the twinkling of an eye, they had me measured, with templates of cloth laid out, rough cut, pinned, and tried on before we left. The four of us enjoyed it immensely and, while waiting for the others, fell into delightful conversation with an elderly British couple and a couple of visiting Australians.

Then we had several blocks of riding through the streets of Kowloon, absorbing the sights that Michael pointed out to us. Kowloon had a peculiar odor, a combination of fish saltwater and burnt almonds. I got rather sick of it after a while. We drove along Nathan

Road and to the Golden Crown Restaurant for a Chinese Sunday breakfast. We understood that this was quite a Sunday custom. It was a large place with several floors and many families with all sorts of children. Pretty little girls carried ovens and pots, and you helped yourself as they came by. You kept your pots or plates and then stacked them beside your place at the table. At the end, they counted the number of plates and charged you accordingly. We had two dozen varieties of food and lots and lots of jasmine tea. The people were very lazy and relaxed, reading their newspapers, visiting from table to table, kids playing on the floor and running around, happy families showing their kin off to each other. It was all very warm and friendly, and one didn't need to speak or understand Chinese to appreciate it. The care and affection the Chinese have for their children and the respect that age seemed to command were impressively obvious.

Then we went to a jewelry shop, a camera shop, and finally to the Ocean Terminal Building where we were overwhelmed with shops. We made some individual purchases of jade earrings, gold chains, Chinese pajamas, tape recorders, etc.

Julie left us, and Michael then took us on a terrific sight-seeing tour. We drove around Kowloon some more, then caught the Star Ferry across the bay to Hong Kong Island. The bay was filled with ships of all sorts. Hong Kong Island had a dreadful fish smell downtown. There we took the cable car to Victoria Peak, Michael drove his car up, and we met him. We drove around the peak, looking at the scenery. The view of the bay and Kowloon is just marvelous. I thrill each time I view it. I believe that Hong Kong is one of the most fascinating harbor cities of the world, and the sights are so many and varied that I never know which are more interesting. We drove to the Tigar Balm Gardens. This is an Oriental Fantasia built on the fortunes of a Chinese Vicks VapoRub and Ben-Gay. We toured the Aw Boon House with its glorious collection of jade in kinds and colors one wouldn't have believed existed. We drove around the mountainside, past fascinating villas and homes along the streets. This was quite an unnerving experience, for they drive on the left-hand side, and Michael's car had a right-hand steering wheel. This got a little hairy, seeing everyone on the wrong side of the road. We wound down to the backside of Hong Kong Island to Repulse Bay and its famous hotel. On the beach, we drank Philippine San Miguel beer, and relaxed, took pictures, and wrote cards. Then we went back through Aberdeen and the Junk Fleet City. We took the ferry back to Kowloon and returned to the tailor of Mayland on Lock Road for our fittings.

I was absolutely amazed by the work and found out that probably two people in some little loft had been working all day to cut and sew and now had produced two really elegant special suits for a mere 550 Hong Kong dollars ($98 U.S.) that would have cost me $500 at home. Julie took us by her sweater shop, and I selected a handmade beauty to be shipped home to my wife.

We then went to the hotel and, over martinis, recapitulated the day and laid plans for the evening.

A walk in the evening air brought us back through the crowded, bustling streets to the Peninsula. Here we washed, cleaned up, and dressed. Then we all met in the lobby, and Michael and Julie drove us out of town into the hills of the New Territories to the Carlton Hotel. Here we sat eating an interesting Chinese dinner, with a spectacular view of Kowloon below us all lit up. The crab meat, corn soup, and jasmine tea had a peculiar smell and taste that I couldn't quite get myself to fully enjoy. I thought I'd had enough jasmine tea to last me a lifetime. I began to feel that I was not really very fond of Chinese cuisine. I thought this is a hell of a time to decide that!

The entertainment was a Filipino dance band and singer, but none of us felt that energetic. We drove back down a winding mountain road, stopping along the way to look at Kai Tak Airport, another spectacular sight: A piece of dark jade outlined with small green emeralds jutting out into a blue sapphire bay—a very pretty sight.

We were sad to say good-night and good-bye to this most pleasant couple. Michael was a former Nationalist Chinese army officer of fourteen years' service who chose not to go to Taiwan, but to remain in Kowloon running his tailoring shop. He and Julie have one adopted thirteen-year-old daughter. They certainly could not have been more helpful, kind, or generous.

17

Although it was getting late, we decided to go down to the Pesa Bar, the discotheque at the hotel. We were joined by Tatem and proceeded to combine Filipino San Miguel beer with Paddy Irish whiskey into a wild type of Oriental boilermaker.

The music was "I'm a Coming Home Soldier," "Strangers in the Night," "Georgie Girl," "I'm a Believer," and "Snoopy and the Red Baron." Sam immediately took up with the last song and wandered around, singing it from table to table and repeatedly requesting it to be played. We probably had it played ten times during the night, and he became the Red Baron!

The disco was filled largely with young people of all nationalities. I was surprised at the number of young Americans and wondered what they were doing there? Of course, before the evening was over, we had gotten into a number of heated arguments over American involvement in Vietnam. It was again most disturbing to be taken to task for going to help out. I was very impressed by the cynicism of the young Australian disk jockey. She could easily have been my daughter and was one of the most vociferous voices directed at our group of old-men-volunteer doctors: "The war was a waste of time and the United States could not win." The local Chinese whom we had met felt the same way. Most encouraging! She kept playing Roy Orbinson's "And There Won't Be Many Coming Home."

After the Red Baron was thoroughly plastered and we had emptied the bar and there was no more music, we managed to get to bed.

CHAPTER FOUR

SAIGON

The Pearl (Paris) of the Orient

Again after a night of very little sleep, I was awakened by the telephone call and had a well-deserved headache. A hot and cold shower improved that. I tested my self-laundered, drip-dry shirt (the first trial) and found it O.K. We all settled our accounts, breakfasted, and then the limousines took us up to Kai Tak where we reversed the procedures with ticket check, baggage turn-in, customs, and immigration.

We boarded an Air Cathay, four-engine Electra and at 9:15 took off into the drizzling, rainy overcast for a three-hour flight to Saigon.

I had a window seat and a new companion. Ernie said, as they passed out the cocktails, "I never drink until after five, but I never know what time it really is anymore!" So we settled back with martinis and waited for our Peking duck in orange sauce. My internal, body-timing mechanism was so fouled up that I felt never would I get myself straightened out as to what time it was again. I had lost track of the days of the week or days of the month.

As we were finishing dinner with orange tea (thankfully not Jasmine) at 11:15, we crossed over the coast of South Vietnam from the South China Sea. At noon, we sat down on Ton Son Nhut airport, and we were in "Nam."

The first thing that really got me was the heat. As you stepped from the air-conditioning of the airplane out of the door, the heat slapped you in the face and body as if you had walked into a blast furnace. Within minutes, I was sweat-soaked, and it took me a couple of weeks to get to where I wasn't always conscious of being very hot.

Upon our arrival, we were met by Dr. Malcolm E. Phelps, a tall, gangling, big man with a shining bald head and an easy manner. He had us all pose in front of the air terminal for pictures (which I never saw) and cautioned us alarmingly, "Don't let anybody carry your bag for you!" We picked up our sixty-six pounds per individual and panted and perspired through the passport, immigration, and customs areas. Again, I had to open my suitcase—guess I looked suspicious or something!

The terminal was a long, low building, quite open in all areas with the damndest sea of humanity milling about. There was a peculiar, identifiable odor about the place, which I noted again in later years and which indelibly marked Ton Son Nhut on my brain. I think it was a combination of human sweat, plus a muggy, damp,

19

swamp smell plus a damp, concrete smell, with perhaps the odor of some kind of plant (maybe food or bushes) added in. Anyhow, it assailed the nostrils and was not exactly unpleasant, just pungently singular.

We somehow pushed and made our way through all of this to a bus waiting outside. It was a leftover public-school type of bus with the windows open, but covered with close-knit, heavy wire. Dr. Phelps increased our beginning anxieties by pointing out, "The wire will keep grenades from being tossed in! Also, don't stick your arms out as someone will surely come by on a bike and steal your watch!"

We drove through a literally war-torn city to 191 Cong Ly, the USAID guest house. The house or villa sat directly on the street and was entered through a closed gate, manned by a Vietnam civilian who closed it and locked it after we entered. It made you wonder.

As we got to our destination, the driver stopped the bus on a side street just at its corner junction with Cong Ly. Dr. Phelps told us to sit still. He got out and trotted a distance down the main street, looked into some gates, and came back. Then he told us each to grab our suitcases and then singly, in a crouching run, to scoot down the street and turn in at the open gates. A couple of the men did this sort of lackadaisically, and Doctor Phelps yelled, "Run, run, get down, get down, hurry!" He was like a top sergeant sending his men over the top! For a bunch of middle-aged men, huffing and puffing, sweat rolling down, our hearts pounding from anxiety and fear, we did remarkably well and were soon inside the gates of the villa. (Later, they merely drove the bus inside!) (Welcome to Vietnam: unbelievable!)

We unloaded and went into the main living-room area, and everyone grabbed a seat on the floor. Dr. Phelps had the beer broken out all around. It was American and not very cool. No one was particularly hungry, as we had eaten just a few hours before. We were hot, which made intestinal activity sluggish, and were becoming more apprehensive, which tightened up our innards even more.

There were a number of paperwork forms to fill out. We were given our name tags in Vietnamese, with *Bac Si* in prominent letters. Dr. Phelps was aided by an assistant, John Miller, an aggressive, pleasant, young man. Then we settled back for a briefing. Both Dr. Phelps and John spoke alternately. They were earnest, but tried to keep it light. I felt they wanted to be serious without frightening us.

One of the first questions we wanted to ask was about the danger.

"Dangerous? Probably less than you may think. More than 100 doctors had made the trip by mid '66 and no one had been wounded."

"Don't go around in big bunches or groups, but certainly don't go out by yourself. If something happens, don't go running toward the event. Stay away or out of big crowds. And be in your hotel by 11 P.M." I thought that was certainly an interesting comment on visiting a foreign country. Then they continued. "Don't give money to children; protect your wallets in crowds, pickpockets are thick as flies. Don't pay what is asked for: bargain for everything, even the price of the cyclo ride." They told us about several places, none of which meant anything and I forgot them.

Dr. Phelps impressed on us in no uncertain terms: "First and foremost, you are here to win friends for the United States and, secondly, to treat sick people." (And in that order!) "Everytime we treat one of these people, he is more oriented toward us than toward Communism."

We were cautioned not to be drinking the water. Everyone drank beer or soda pop; Bireley's orange drink was evidently a big seller, along with a weak 7-Upish-like lemon soda.

"Welcome to Saigon and Vietnam," they said!

Then we were driven around to the USAID headquarters building where we exchanged money. Again we went through a gate opened and closed by a Vietnamese in military clothing and another who had a mirror device mounted on a long pole, with which he scanned the undersurface of the bus.

"Just looking to make certain no bombs have been attached!" we were told. I wondered how that would be possible at all, as the bus had been backed inside the Cong Ly villa compound for the several hours we were there. But then I had something to learn.

The exchange rate was 118 P (piasters) for one United States dollar, and I got twenty dollars in Vietnamese money. Also, we each got military payment certificates (MPC's), which were the military money on a dollar-for-dollar basis. We had been cautioned about getting too much cash, and most of us had practically everything in travelers' checks.

"Don't worry, you won't have much to spend it on, anyhow," we were told.

There was not enough room at the Cong Ly guest house for all of us, plus those expected doctors who would be coming in from the provinces after finishing their tours. So six of us had been assigned to another hotel and after getting our money changed, we were driven to the Hotel Vo Tanh. The group was Miller, Bob S., Ernie Tatem, myself, and Marshall. The last-named doctor had just come in from Go Cong and was on his way home.

We had a great deal of trouble about our room. It seemed as if we were not the group they had been expecting. Because of the language barrier, we couldn't figure out whether it was the number of people, the date, or us. I don't know how they could have known about us individually or why it should have made any difference. However, we were firm and said we wanted our rooms, and somehow they were forthcoming: on the fifth floor (walk-up)! There were several kids lolling around through all this, and they were eager to carry our bags upstairs. I personally was rather thankful. The two boys who got my sixty-six pounds upstairs waited for an obvious tip, but I didn't know exactly how much or how to figure out the coins. What I finally gave one boy didn't seem to make him happy. Several of them sort of milled around in my room looking and waiting. I finally had to literally "shoo" them out of the room.

The room was small, bare, of white plaster, with dirty walls and ceiling with a big, old barbershop type fan. There was an "air conditioner" in the window that was really only a fan. There was some 1930 wooden furniture. No rugs and keys to everything, but none of them worked for any door! Quite a comedown from the Peninsula!

Three of us had rooms together facing an opening onto a balcony. There was a shower and a commode that flushed.

I walked out onto the balcony and was slapped in the face by the most god-awful view of the city or whatever it was. As far as I could see were dingy, partially-built buildings, tin roofs, sheds, smoke, crowds of people, thousands of cyclos, motorcycles, and bicycles, and the noise and smell.

I wrote home, "Darling, you wouldn't believe it! What an awful place this is. It reminds me in appearance, smell and feel of Manila in 1945 except for one thing: There the Filipinos were on our side and here apparently you can trust no one!"

I shaved, put on cooler clothes, and got some letters together, just in case I found somewhere to mail them. We trudged down the stairs, dying of thirst—afraid of the water. No kind of vending machines or restaurants were available. The USAID bus came by at 7:45 with the rest of the group and drove us all out to Cholon, the Chinese quarter of Saigon.

There at Fuigi's, an outdoor Japanese restaurant, run by a Filipino, we Americans had a Chinese dinner, our first meal in Vietnam. With a little practice, I got the hang of the chopsticks and eventually learned the secret of their use. We gobbled down the sweet corn, crab soup, pork and almonds, fried shrimp with varied sauces, and the inevitable egg roll (Vietnamese type, of course). A particularly tasty course was the *Bo Bay Mon* or beef in seven dishes: Each dish with beef and differing vegetables and each with a special sauce.

Dr. Phelps had brought along two of the Vietnamese office girls and Dr. Yuan from the Saigon medical-school facility. He spoke good English and was well educated. The waiters of course were Vietnamese, and I was amazed at the small size of people. As time went along, I found them to be reserved, courteous, small but well proportioned, intensely loyal to family, and respectful of the aged.

The next morning, after a sound night's sleep of seven hours, I was beginning to feel better. I had begun to think I'd never get a real night's sleep again. Here it was Tuesday, and the last time I remembered going to bed like a real person was Thursday.

It had been a long time since I had used a straight razor, but I was beginning to get the hang of it.

About 8:30 that morning, the bus finally came to pick up the six of us hungry and thirsty and took us to the USAID Headquarters (Mondial Hotel) where the "mirror man" looked us "over" (i.e., under) again. Certainly an encouraging action. We all wondered what would really happen if he saw something.

Our meeting room was six flights up (no elevator), and Dr. Phelps took them two at a time. We should have been warned to get ourselves in condition before doing all this! The brochure had only specified: "A need for men in good health . . . able to withstand the rigors of tropical cimate." It failed to mention backpacking up and down hotel steps!

We were briefed by various sorts on the political and geographic, and were given some history of the country and some explanation of the USAID/USOM organization and how the VPVN program fitted into it. The present status of the war situation was lightly touched. (I guess so as not to alarm us.) About 11 o'clock, they said that was all. We were dismissed and scheduled to meet at 4 P.M. at 191 Cong Ly. We all stumbled down the six flights and stepped onto the streets.

After twenty-four hours of being scared to death about every move, we now suddenly found we were all alone somewhere in the middle of this disastrous city and on our own!

At first, we were hesitant about taking off around town. Anyhow, we soon screwed up our courage and plunged into the mass of humanity that twenty-four hours a day made up Saigon.

Saigon was called the Paris of the Orient because of the wide boulevards shaded by tall, exotic trees. It was fifty-one square miles on the west bank of the Saigon River and actually dated back only about 200 years to a lowly fishing village. It now had two million inhabitants.

We walked down Lei Long to the marketplace—absolutely unbelievable: the traffic, bicycles, cars, people, and refugees had literally exploded the city. The streets were torn up and badly in need of repair. The dust, noise, heat, confusion, and commotion were beyond belief. And people, people everywhere. Two of us "lost" fountain pens out of our shirt pockets before we'd gone a hundred yards!

We had been warned to take off elastic-band watches and keep them together with our wallets in a side pocket, with our hands in there too!

Every time we stopped to look at something or to get our bearings or figure out how to get across one of the traffic circles, kids and people crowded around, grabbing and touching at our bare arms and hands and clothes, talking and jabbering away. Of course, we couldn't understand, and they couldn't (or wouldn't) speak English.

We found our way to Tu-Do (Liberty Street), the main street, and to Cho Ben Tanh (the Central Market). Here there were stands or stalls with silks, brocade, rattan, straw, bamboo, brass, fruits, lacquer ware, ceramics, and bronze ware. All of these articles were obtained by bargaining or haggling about the price.

On Nguyen-Hue Street, we walked through the flower markets. We explored the markets along Lei Long and the Street of Flowers. It was like pictures of India I'd remembered seeing years ago. We found the USO (they actually still had it going this long after World War II!) and thankfully got inside from the heat and confusion for a while, for a Coke and information.

Leaving the USO, we were walking down the street, about to cross over. Sort of leaning against a post, we spotted an obviously American civilian among the hundreds of surrounding "little yellow people." We hailed him, and it turned out that he was Dr. Bob Cook, a general practitioner from Cincinnati, just finishing his tour at Danang.

He said, "I know just what you fellows need." We followed him to the Caravelle Hotel where there was an American-style restaurant up on top, and we finally got something to eat. He was very helpful, showing us around the area, telling us tales of his tour, and commenting on the war situation in general.

After lunch, three of us, Bob Sookey, Bob Green, and I hired a car for 100 P each, and the driver took us all over Saigon. We never really knew where we were or were going because we certainly didn't understand the language, and it seemed the driver really knew very little English. We could identify the Roman Catholic cathedral and the presidential palace. There were pagodas everywhere. Interestingly, I came to learn Vietnam was a rather religious country with a free choice of religion. The Buddhist monks, in their orange and yellow robes with their begging bowls, were the obvious symbols of the major religion of the country, Buddhism. Christianity was largely Roman Catholic and, in the South, we saw the fathers with their collars and habited sisters. Protestants and evangelical Christians were there, but not to a great degree. There were also Confucians, Muhammadans, and the weird, peculiar Cao Dai, a blend of Confucianism, Taoism, Buddhism, and Christianity!

We finally got the driver to get us to 191 Cong Ly.

At 4 o'clock, we all reassembled and had a further briefing and got our assignments. A worrisome note was the fact they took our passports and said they would return them later. We were warned not to skip about the country, "visiting," but to stay with our assignments. We were not to return to Saigon until notified. Our tickets and visas for the return flight would be ready then. So we ended up stuck wherever we were going to be and without a passport; we couldn't go anywhere!

Feeling braver now in small groups, we got out on the streets, haggled for cyclos, and took off downtown.

A group of us stopped off at the Continental Hotel where there was the fabulous open porch-plaza type bar: twenty-foot-high ceilings with old-fashioned, wooden, ceiling fans, wooden furniture with tablecloths, and white-coated Chinese waiters. Absolutely fantastic. A movie set couldn't have done it better—the crossroads of the Orient, drinking their evening gin and tonic; well-dressed, chic Western women walking clipped French poodles; bearded, mustachioed English types; civilians, army, navy, air force; GI's in combat gear with sidearms and carbines; Indians, Chinese, and Vietnamese. All sitting, talking, and drinking. One half expected to see Ernest Hemingway or Robert Ruark stroll in! The only thing lacking was a couple of Cary Grant French Foreign Legionnaires. We drank Vietnamese beer and listened to Foster Marshall, an orthopedic surgeon from Columbia, South Carolina, just back from Go Gong in the Delta area. He had a lot to tell about the work, the people, and getting along.

Afterward, we walked over to the Rex Hotel, which was the American Army BOQ. On the rooftop restaurant, we had a steak dinner.

After that, we walked around and went down to the waterfront. Long lines of army trucks and tanks rolled down the streets. We saw the German hospital ship, S.S. *Helgoland*. It had been there since 1966, receiving a lot of good publicity for its work with the civilians, especially children.

Then we went to the Majestic Hotel for a beer at their rooftop bar. We sat and looked out over the Saigon River and city lights, listening to the artillery boom and the light flashes from air strikes in the Iron Triangle area about thirty-five miles to the north. It was all so unreal. My father would never have believed all this!

Marshall and I walked back to our hotel building, holding on to our wallets as curfew time came on. We had a few anxious moments a couple of times when we were unsure of our direction, but somehow made it.

For the next morning, we had been told to get up early and be ready to leave at 5:45. Everyone was being taken to TSN to catch a plane. I got up at 5:00. By 9 o'clock, no one had showed. We were fuming, cussing, and wondering, not knowing whether to try to get over to the USAID Headquarters or to the Cong Ly guest house—both in opposite directions—carrying our bags! Finally, a young man on a bicycle arrived, cheerily announced in a casual manner that the bus driver went to the wrong hotel and we would have to wait until tomorrow! Then he tooled off. Needless to say, the five of us were much exasperated!

So we were "free" for another day of sight-seeing. After a long stroll, arriving at Cong Ly, I took a nap on the couch, for the heat, exertion, and lack of sleep were catching up with me.

By now, I was brave enough to catch a pedicab (pousse). These three-wheeled, pedal-propelled, armchairs had a minimum fare of ten piasters. We were supposed to bargain for the price before the trip. But since we couldn't communicate and we didn't really know where we wanted to go, we ended up paying fifty piasters for our ride "downtown"! We finally got him to the plaza in front of the Roman Catholic cathedral. The plaza had been named in honor of the late president John F. Kennedy and that word (Kennedy) he apparently understood!

We met up with an army psychiatrist from Phu Vinh who was going out on R & R and we all went again to the Rex BOQ for lunch.

Captain Milligans was a nice chap and interesting to talk to about the war.

After lunch, I felt confident enough to take off by myself and find St. Christopher's Anglican Church, but was disappointed to find it locked. There was no one around, although it was just across the street from the British Embassy.

I took a long, dusty, crowded walk down to the waterfront and took many movies.

I found myself again at the S.S. *Helgoland*. I went up the gangplank to ask the German sailor-sentry for permission to go aboard. He was in the process of refusing me (they have so many visitors) when a German doctor just happened to come aboard and, hearing me, took me in tow. He took me up to the officers' lounge and gave me a cup of coffee and a cigarette. He told me I was looking sort of clammy—and I admit I was feeling sort of pale from the heat. Dr. Klaus Wagner was a young, large, blue-eyed blond, who spoke English, French, and some Vietnamese. He had had some training at the University of Pennsylvania. We had a splendid tour around the ship. There were 150 medical and surgical beds, three operating rooms, and intensive care, laboratory, and X-ray. It was a very pleasant few hours, and I did appreciate his kindness.

Then I plunged back into the heat and dust of the streets, past the home of "Our Man in Saigon" (the American Embassy): barricaded, barb-wired, heavily guarded. Then I had a two-mile walk back to the hotel, up five flights, with no electricity, hence, no fan. With the door open, the burning smoke, gas fumes, and sewer stench came. I stripped down and lay down to wait for sunset before showering in order to cool off.

My biggest problem that night was the fact I was parched—thirsty with nothing to drink and no way to get anything. I was certainly afraid of the water, and nothing else was obtainable.

Anyhow, by that night, as I got my letters written and ready to leave early in the morning, I noted in my diary that, "I think I've about got this city mastered and now am ready to get out," and on to our jobs.

CHAPTER FIVE

RACH GIA

Clouds heavy on high hills,
Birds slide down, darkness:
The waves are memory.
Too dark to see
And yet I am sick for home.

The Long River
—Huy Can

Flying over the Delta of Vietnam as the sun came up was a gorgeous sight. The Mekong and Bassac rivers meander and curve through a sea of green, twisting like snakes, with many tributaries. They flow from Cambodia, eventually emptying into the South China Sea. The entire pattern is crisscrossed by canals, and the area is easily visible from two thousand feet at 150 miles per hour. The air was clear and the ride smooth. The Air America pilot in the twin engine Dornier was also the steward and yelled back that we would find hot coffee in the thermos. So we helped ourselves, and after a couple of cups and a cigarette, I felt better, for there had been no breakfast and we'd been up a long time.

We had rolled out at five o'clock with some Vietnamese-type pounding on our doors (our wake-up call!), hastily dressed, and having never unpacked, were ready to go. This day, the bus got there, although one hour late. (I was beginning to get the picture; this war sort of moved along without too much compulsiveness.)

We rattled through all sorts of dark streets until we found ourselves again at Ton Son Nhut and the strange smell. An American guide (unknown) took us to the Air American counter, got our tickets, which was actually signing us on a manifest, which actually was only writing our names down on a scratch piece of paper, done by the pilot! The pilot was an American in civilian clothes, but wore a flak jacket and carried a carbine. We five passengers exchanged glances of wonderment. It wasn't exactly your everyday little feeder airline service back home!

29

We all climbed aboard the small twin and straddled cans and boxes. By then, daylight was breaking, and we had what seemed to be an interminable taxi trip down the flight line. There was every conceivable type of airplane civilian, military, singles, twins, jets, L-19's, Caribous, Beeches, Hercs, and the inevitable choppers. (As in later years, I found we couldn't have waged this war without the helicopter. They were omnipresent.)

After forty-five minutes, we put down in Can Tho, and everyone got off. D. J. Miller was to stay here.

The Air American Airline was like something out of "Terry and the Pirates" (only quite serious). They sort of made up their schedule as they went along. The pilot had to take some of the cargo and a couple of passengers to Vinh Binh and come back to Cantho, so I got off to report to the IV Corps USAID Headquarters group.

The USAID representative, Jordan, met us in lieu of his two superiors, Douglas and Marsh, who were out visiting some of the villages. He took us to the province hospital where I got my first glimpse of civilian medical care, Vietnamese-style in wartime.

We met Major Frank Camp, the aggressive, young air force surgeon, who ran the air force surgical team assigned there and had evidently made quite a reputation for himself during the prior year. He showed us the first mitral commissurotomy patient operated on in Vietnam just three days before. There was a Korean medical team and an augmenting USAID physician team to fill in the gaps. The hospital had some nurses and a nurse anesthetist. The condition of the wards and grounds was evidently high by Vietnamese standards, but my diary comment was "ugh!" We visited the prison ward where we saw the Black Pajama Boys (VC) who were receiving the same treatment as all the other Vietnamese.

I was the only passenger on the next leg to Rach Gia and rode in the copilot's seat for the forty-minute flight. The Americans in Rach Gia did not know exactly when I would be arriving—telephone communications were so poor. It had taken the Can Tho USAID office three hours to get a message through to the province hospital the day before to inform them I wasn't coming. I was interested later on to find out that no one on the American team ever received any word as to my arriving or not. (It made you wonder who took what telephone message and did what with it?) The only information the Rach Gia medical team had was that around the end of the month or first of the next month, a civilian doctor, most likely a surgeon, would appear. No name, specific date, or time!

The only really safe travel and communication was by air.

Kien Giang Province lay in the southwestern sector of the Mekong Delta. Cambodia bordered the northwest, and the Gulf of Siam formed the southern border. To the east was the U Minh forest, a longtime impenetrable bastion of the Vietcong.

Rach Gia was the province capital. It was a town of an estimated 30,000 people, located at the mouth of the Son Ahon River on the Gulf of Siam, and was primarily a fishing community. The one hospital to serve the entire province was located here.

We landed outside of town at a well-established, although unpaved, single dirt strip. It was about five miles from town and was called the "Long Strip," I later learned. This is where the twin-engine Caribous could land to bring in supplies. As there was no one there, we waited around a while and still no one came. So the pilot took off, and we circled over the town (it was bigger than I'd anticipated). He buzzed the hospital a couple of times, and we returned to the Long Strip and waited. About thirty minutes later, a jeep with two nurses in fatigues screeched up, and there was much "We didn't know what happened to you," "We didn't know when you were coming," "Whether it would be the Short Strip or Long Strip," "We haven't heard a thing," etc.

Part of the confusion was further engendered by the fact that they were also expecting a visiting group of army doctors from the MACV Headquarters in Saigon and didn't know whether I was in this group or not.

We introduced around, and I threw my suitcase in the back and we speeded back into town. The nurse who drove seemed to have but two speeds: fast and stop! We churned the dust on the roads.

Arriving at the hospital, they drove to our quarters, the doctor's house. Here I was introduced around and given a room.

My roommate was Captain Bill Irish of the United States Air Force who was the anesthesiologist for the team. We were "roomies" for only one week before his year's tour was over and he left, so I did not get to know him very well. Also, my first few days, so much was going on and so many new things occurring, we didn't have much time to talk.

As a matter of fact, the present team were all at the end of their year's tour and within a few weeks had been totally replaced by the new team that I really came to know.

I wasn't particularly hungry and had arrived a little late for lunch anyhow. All the getting settled and looking around occupied several hours, and about this time the aforementioned MACV "doctor inspectors" arrived for a tour of the hospital conducted by Commander John LeB., the U.S. Navy surgeon who was the medical-team chief.

Three hours after arriving, at 3 P.M., I guess I went to war.

During the next two hours, twenty-five civilian casualties were brought in. Some were questionably Vietcong, and we operated for the next eight hours. My cases were a leg amputation, two bowel resections and repairs, and one bowel resection and colostomy. All were performed without blood, no history and physical, no laboratory studies or "pre-operative" evaluation! Unbelievable. They lay on stretchers scattered about the emergency room, on the porch and yard leading to the operating suite, and were brought in one after another. The other general surgeon, Navy Lieutenant Dan, operated in one room and I in the other. Commander LeB. triaged in the waiting area and did debridements and fractures.

At midnight, I was tired, hungry, sleepy, aching, confused, and amazed, but this was what I'd come to do and I knew it was right.

CHAPTER SIX

THE HOSPITAL

Beer in a huge jar.
A chicken. I offer them to you.
Take them to our mothers, our fathers,
Our uncles, our mothers' brothers,
Live near the Arch of Heaven
Be happy in the Caverns of Death.

—*Vietnamese Peasants Funeral Song*

The hospital and its environs were the center of my life for the next two months. It literally was my only life, except for a few side excursions to be described later.

The hospital was located on the Northwest side of the Son Ahon River as it opened into the Gulf of Siam (Thailand). The back of the hospital was about 100 feet from the seawall, and the front was facing a partially paved street that eventually led to downtown. The hospital was of one- and two-story, low, rambling, colonial construction, having been built about 1880–1890 with no changes since and evidently not much upkeep in recent years.

The hospital site plan was that of an open pavilion (the fourteen buildings arranged in a rectangle) surrounding a central courtyard. The entire area covered about the equivalent of two or three city blocks. Running down the east side of the hospital was a dirty, dusty, narrow road, lined with a few huts that backed up against the river. At the end of this street was the building, a more or less modern one-and-a-half story structure that was the living quarters of the males of the team, the mess hall for all of the team, and the recreation center for the entire MAAG group, the Bac Si House.

Entering the hospital from the town street entrance, one passed through barbed-wire fencing and a gate. Passing a guardhouse, you went between the administration building and the dental clinic. (No dentist, however.) One was then in the large, open courtyard, a plaza full of trees, park, and gardens—really quite pretty and charming, except for the heat and the smell. Along both sides were two-story, old, yellow-stuccoed buildings, with open porches facing the inside of the rectangle. These were the hospital wards and at the ends of each were two small rooms for sort of private accommodations. The front half of the hospital was given over to medical patients. Midway down the riverside was the obstetrical building, beyond that a female surgical ward, and finally the military ward. This was about opposite our quarters, and I could walk over and through a porch between the military and female surgical wards and be in the hospital compound proper. On the other side of the compound beyond the medical ward buildings was the male surgical ward, the jail ward, and the pediatric ward at the end. Completing the compound square at the far end was the postoperative ward.

In the middle of the compound toward the far end were two separate small buildings: the furthermost one was the emergency room, laboratory, and X-ray department combined, and the nearer one was the surgical suite, recovery room, and central supply.

All of the wards and surgical and emergency buildings were connected by covered walks and porches.

A typical ward was a large, open room with a high ceiling, containing about forty beds side by side in rows along the wall with a central aisle. The doors were open and unscreened, and the windows were open and unscreened. The floors were tiled, cracking, and needing repair. Each bed had arrangements for the erection of a mosquito netting at nighttime. Most of the beds were wooden, with no mattress or springs and only a bamboo net covered with a sheet. (My children, later seeing some of the slides, commented about there being no blankets: not needed in the constant heat!) There were often two, three, or four patients in a bed. The patient's family slept under the bed or on the porches. The relatives were the nurses rather than the R.N.'s! The toilets were of the communal privy type in the back of each ward outside. Located at strategic areas around the compound were several pumps where the water was obtained. Open concrete gutters ran along the sidewalks and outside the wards and crisscrossed the compound. Patients would line up and relieve themselves in the open ditches! Unbelievable! Refuse (human, animal, and plant) was swept into these where it lay until the rainy season came along and washed it all into the neighboring canal or river on either side! (It didn't rain while I was there.)

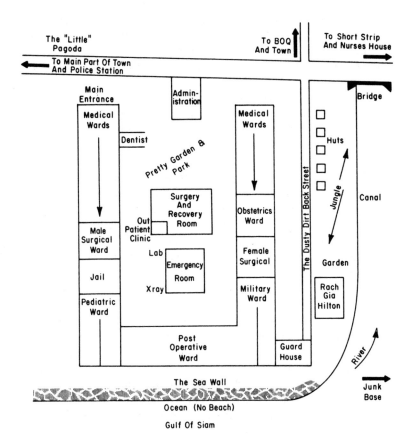

The "Little" Pagoda

To BOQ And Town

To Short Strip And Nurses House

To Main Part Of Town And Police Station

Main Entrance

Admin-istration

Bridge

Medical Wards

Medical Wards

Dentist

Huts

Pretty Garden & Park

Surgery And Recovery Room

Obstetrics Ward

The Dusty Dirt Back Street

Jungle

Canal

Out Patient Clinic

Male Surgical Ward

Lab

Emergency Room

Female Surgical

Garden

Jail

Xray

Military Ward

Rach Gia Hilton

Pediatric Ward

Post Operative Ward

Guard House

River

The Sea Wall

Junk Base

Ocean (No Beach)

Gulf Of Siam

Kien Giang Province Hospital (Not To Scale)
(Walkways, Covered Walks, Out Buildings,
And Latrines Omitted)

If this seems crude and unsanitary, it was! As I was to find out, sanitation and public health would do more for the Vietnamese people than a few hundred doctors operating on a few thousand patients! (As in the real world and history in general, one-on-one medicine is nice, humane, and Christian; but more lives have been saved by preventive medicine and public health measures the world around.)

There was no isolation of communicable diseases. It was thought that the Vietnamese had an immunity from the litter, refuse, garbage, dirt, etc., and didn't infect each other! Fantastic! The Westerners were immunologic virgins!

The surgery suite was a more recently completed building. It was entered through a screened door (and a solid door capable of being locked) from a covered walk off the emergency room. One walked into an open receiving or holding area, from which five doors to as many rooms opened. The first on the left was a motel-sized room that was used for the outpatient clinic. The second was a larger room, the central or sterile supply room, where the instruments and gowns were autoclaved. Directly ahead, at the end of the building, were two operating rooms, one on the left and one on the right. These were the only two rooms in the entire hospital that had air-conditioning units, and the one in the room on the right never did work! The scrub sink was located between the two rooms. Continuing the swing around the interior of the building, the last room and to the right was the postoperative ward, containing six beds and a window. (For the families to look inside!)

The space behind the emergency room and surgery buildings was given over to a garden. It was supposedly a vegetable garden, and it probably says something about the Sisters when one realized it was largely flowers! Next to the garden was a giant, concrete cistern for catching fresh rainwater that was the emergency water-storage supply! (It didn't rain during my time there.) There were scattered, high, palm trees with large coconuts and then, further along, a parklike area of mango trees—big trees with lots of shade, eternally green. I often wondered what kind of outlook on life one would have living where the vegetation was always the same color.

The emergency room was a single, large, open room, with

several little areas and a "minor operating" table. Off of this was the laboratory where about the most that could be obtained was a complete blood count and urinalysis. Blood chemistry studies, blood electrolyte, and gas studies were simply not available. The X ray was a portable machine that could take extremity bone films and chest X rays. Even the simplest barium contrast studies were non-existent!

The hospital had at one time been run by a French Roman Catholic order, and there were still a few of the Sisters left. I had contact only with the superior, Sister Clotilde, who, in her French, broken-English speech, was very charming, but severe and retiring. The Sisters fixed the rice for the basic meal distribution twice daily. There were a few Vietnamese civilian nurses (the approximate equivalent of our registered nurses), but most of the help were aides. (Most of the real nursing care was given by the families.)

The surgical service (100 beds) had only *two* Vietnamese nurses. The next morning after my arrival, the surgeons took me on rounds to have a look at the patients. They tried to at least walk by every patient at least once each week! With three surgeons who spent their mornings operating, their afternoon in clinics seeing outpatients, and nights doing emergency operations, there wasn't much time left to see the 150 surgical patients in the beds of the wards! If one started operating Monday morning, by Wednesday night you couldn't remember what you'd done or find the patient! Unbelievable. All the doctors we talked to before coming had told us the same thing and said, "You won't believe it!" and we didn't until we saw it and experienced it ourselves!

During the course of our walk, I met Dr. Tuan, the *medicine-chef* (chief doctor) of the hospital. As a matter of fact, there were only two physicians for this entire 600-bed hospital with over 800 patients (two in a bed). Both of these doctors had private practices and private clinics in the downtown area! So one can imagine how much medical care the average patient was getting. Continuing, Dr. Tuan, who was receptive to Western medicine, was also the medical chief for the province of Kien Giang, and he and the other Vietnamese doctor were the only two doctors for the entire province of 350,000. Unbelievable! (They said we wouldn't believe it!)

Dr. Tuan had an *placenta praevia* obstetrical case, and so I did an emergency cesarean section and, without blood, had a live mother and healthy baby boy by lunchtime! Fantastic.

CHAPTER SEVEN

FRIDAY, FEBRUARY THIRD

On the crumbling hills: a wind, another,
with village noises,
Buying, Selling.
Sun cuts down, sky goes up forever.
Long River. Great Sky. No one along the shore.

The Long River
—Huy Can

The Friday afternoon after I had arrived earlier that week was the first time I'd ventured outside the hospital. After attending the surgical clinic and lining up some elective surgical cases for the beginning of the next week, I walked into downtown with Don Hopping, the navy surgeon, and Bill Irish, the air force anesthesiologist.

"Downtown" was about six blocks away and not a bad walk. I got to enjoy it as the days went by. Leaving our doctor house (the "Rach Gia Hilton") at the back of the hospital, one could either walk down the little, dirty, dusty back road to the main cross street or cut through the hospital compound and come out at what I later found out was the front of the hospital. About a half block down the street on the other side was a large pagoda, evidently quite active, for there was always a great deal of coming and going, and the yellow-robed monks were always around. Located in some relation to this was a school, and kids loved to run up to us Americans, tug at our clothes, and rub our skin. (They liked the feel of the hairy arms!) Their teachers or leader would shoo them away, and the children would quickly and laughingly obey.

One of the earliest things I observed about the Vietnamese was their behavior toward children. They seemed to spoil them outrageously, and it was as if everyone looked after everyone else's children also! In reverse, the children seemed to really mind the parental authority, whether their own parents, someone else's parents, teachers, police, or whoever, and all very good naturedly and laughingly.

Passing the pagoda and school at the end of the street was a plaza, with about six streets radiating from it. At the head of this was an imposing, barricaded, barb-wired building, the police station. It was more of a paramilitary type of organization, and there were always jeeps with soldiers and jeeps with machine guns buzzing in and out. A couple of armored personnel carriers were generally backed around. Down a main street leading away from this plaza, three blocks away, was the main market.

This was "downtown." The market was about two blocks long and two blocks wide, surrounded by a circumferential street. The market was closed overhead and open around all sides. Inside, it was divided into areas where the farmers and merchants displayed and sold their wares. It was always a mass of people dressed all alike! (it seemed): sandaled feet, black pajama pants, white blouse shirt, and conical straw hats. All gesticulating, moving, jabbering, yelling—noisy and dusty.

Everyone walked in the streets and shared them with the bicycles, cyclos, pedicabs, jeeps, and occasional aged French cars. On the other side of the street all around from the market were shops of different kinds. One was always barely being missed by the little women with their *Don Ganhs*. These were two wicker baskets suspended from a bamboo pole carried across the shoulders. I guess half of Vietnam was moved this way! Fantastic!

Passing beyond the main market, one was then on the waterfront formed by the large canal that bisected the town. On the market side of the canal were two other very important markets: on one side was the dried-fish market and across the street was the wet-fish market. In order to cross the bridge across the canal, one had to pass between this Scylla and Charybdis like Odysseus.

Crossing the canal, one came into a park area. Here I encountered the first of many fascinating Vietnamese variations on an American theme: there was only one twelve-inch, black-and-white television set in the entire province, and here in the park it was mounted on a ten-foot-high pedestal, flickering and streaked with

39

fades and snowstorms, but surrounded always, always by two or three hundred people looking and listening!

I must admit I was just fascinated. It was so unbelievable! One time, I recognized Premier Thieu, another time a war series, and another time what must have been a movie. But I really didn't tarry very long!

The street split into a one-way set, one going around the park and the other bore off to the left.

If you turned to the right, you would walk a block to the Roman Catholic cathedral and a block further along to another very large open plaza where the bus station was located. This was always a busy place. If one turned extremely to the left, crossing the main canal and before reaching the park, one could walk several blocks down a very pretty, tree-shaded street that paralleled the canal for several blocks until it emptied into the ocean at the site of a truly beautiful and impressive pagoda. (We called it the Big Pagoda.)

After passing around the park and admiring the TV setup, walking another block brought us to a large spacious estate surrounded by a fence and an impressive house set in the midst of some attractive gardens. This was the home of the province chief (like a state governor). There were several APC's parked around, and numerous soldiers and police patrolled the area.

A block further along and we turned down another street that led us to the "important American place in town"!

On one side of the street was a building that housed the headquarters of the USAID activities in the province and other American paramilitay activities. Here also were quarters for the enlisted American military (BEQ I) who were assigned to various military duties with the Military Assistance Command Vietnam (MACV). In addition, and most importantly in order, were also the mail room (for all American and/or foreign, i.e., Third-World people) receiving their mail at this address; the mess hall (American military field ration mess—you knew the food was safe!); and once a week, they had a new movie to show out-of-doors!

Across the street from the BEQI (Bachelor Enlisted Quarters One) was the TOC. This was the Tactical Operating Center of the Military Advisory Assistance Teams (MAAG) and truly the nerve

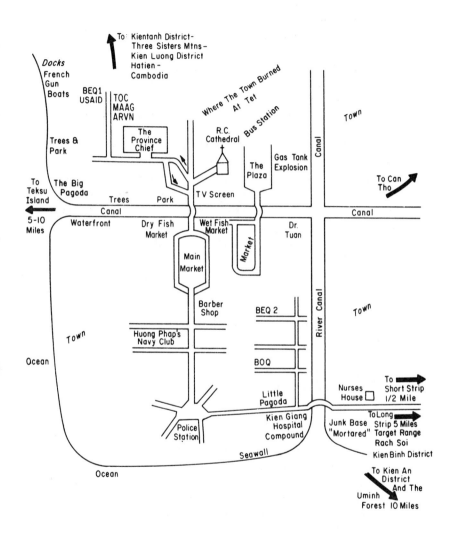

Town of Rach Gia, Capital Kien Giang Province (Not to Scale)

center of what little American military effort there was in the whole area. The communications and operations were found in here, and it was heavily sandbagged, barb-wired, and guarded by Vietnamese and American soldiers.

(The American officers and remainder of enlisted personnel lived in the BOQ and BEQ2 on our side of town, about three blocks from the hospital.)

We stayed and ate supper—I hadn't been eating too well the past few days anyhow and wanted to work up to eating off the economy gradually! I met a number of people with whom I was later to have a great deal of interplay, although I didn't realize it at the time. They all seemed rather surprised at finding a civilian doctor there, but then as one of the Special Forces sergeants (a medic) told me, "Hell, doc, I ain't surprised at anything that happens in this frigging war!" I was beginning to get the picture!

The mentioning of the mail room reminded me how very far away I was from everything and although only a week had passed since I kissed my wife good-bye, it seemed literally like a hundred years! The worst part about it was not being able to pick the phone and call, at least to say "hello." I probably wouldn't have called had I been home, but there was a difference in knowing you absolutely *could not call*! Also, a slowly dawning horror was, wondering what would happen if there were some real emergency that required my presence at home—how would you get out of this place?

I thought to myself, *after only a week you are beginning to have doubts and fears and this is not time to back out*! So I kept my feet warm by some more walking around town as the sun went down and night came on. There wasn't very much anywhere in the way of street lights all over town, and I hurried back home.

During all my time there in Rach Gia, I grew to feel safer than if I'd been on the streets of Washington, D.C., or New York City. I was never molested or threatened, or even put in a situation where I felt I might be. For the most part, I was ignored, passed by, or tolerated. I generally found those with whom I had intimate contact and direct dealings to be very friendly. It was more the situation of a kindly uncle and his doting nieces and nephews. Even the VC seemed to respect us!

CHAPTER EIGHT

THE BLACK PAJAMA BOYS

Now my life is full of hardship—not enough rice to eat nor enough clothing to keep myself warm! But in my heart I keep loyal to the Party and to the people.

—*The Diary of a Viet-Cong Soldier, Do Lac*

The next day after breakfast, we were visited by some U.S. Navy types. They were checking the "local naval base." This was just across the mouth of the river, less than 500 yards from the hospital. Part of the delta's Junk fleet was based here for operations and repairs, and the Vietcong occasionally threw a rocket or mortar shell in there with a frightening explosion and a sudden solitary reminder that the war was omnipresent. Since our medical team was a navy one, the inspectors included that in their tour. I followed around as we toured the hospital, getting a chance to try to learn some of the patients and current problems. Afterward I wired a jaw fracture, ate lunch, then spent the afternoon operating on two casualties who had been hurt in the fighting the day after I arrived, but had not been able to be brought in until today because of Vietcong troops in the area. One had perforating fragment wounds of the stomach, spleen, liver, and pancreas, which I operated on and the other (a young girl) nasty foot and leg wounds that LeBovier did.

After supper, Chief Bill T. had a party consisting of steak (where from?) and champagne (also where from?) as a farewell for their team, all of whose members left during the first ten days after I got there and before the new team arrived.

The party broke up about 10:30, and I went to bed by 11 P.M. I had just gotten to sleep when I heard voices outside my room, "Bac Si come, Bac Si come." The orderlies couldn't get the phone to work, so they came over to the quarters, but didn't know about coming into my room!

Without thinking too much, too quickly, or too deeply, I rolled out of bed, threw on my shirt and pants, and started for the car (as I would back home!). It dawned on me where I was as I crossed the road outside the house and as we strode up the path to the back of the hospital, I was conscious there were three people with me. They were dressed in white hospital-type suits, but I didn't recognize anyone and it was dark. My heart flip-flopped, and I picked up a brisker pace to get inside the emergency room. On the porch outside stood three young-looking men carrying rifles (AK 47s), smoking cigarettes, and saying nothing! Inside in varying positions, attitudes and conditions were six young men, all wearing black pajamas and some with sidearms. They lay on stretchers or sat on the floor scattered about.

I must confess in retrospect after all the years that I cannot believe how naive I was! I had kept up with the war in the newspapers and on television, and I had prepared myself for this trip by studying Bernard Fall's books, but I guess I really didn't think of it as a "war without fronts" (*guerre sans fronts*) and always thought of the enemy as being somebody else—out there or "over there." But to suddenly realize that here I was, a white, a foreigner, a Westerner (French and American were same-same), middle-aged, unarmed, 12,000 miles from home, surrounded at 2 A.M. by the enemy and unable to communicate, gives one something to think about. ("If my daddy could see me now!")

Anyhow, surveying the field, I saw that one had open bones sticking out of the leg. He'd have to go to the operating room, as would another who had abdominal fragment wound holes in his belly. A third one had a couple of bullet holes in an arm, and the other three had minor extremity injuries. I was trying to get them all into the hospital, but the arm-wounded one was negative, and we ended up debriding them with local anesthesia. (Actually, one of the orderlies did this under my direction, and we gave them all penicillin, tetanus, splints, and codeine.) The badly arm-wounded one seemed to be a leader, and he wasn't about to stay, but he didn't seem to mind the two who obviously would. They were all very stoic and unsmiling about the whole proceeding.

I just did what I knew to be the correct surgical management and took the two into the operating suite, after notifying the Vietnamese surgical crew. We operated until 5 A.M. and when the sun came up, the Black-Pajama Boys were gone, and my two patients were in the prison ward with ARVIN soldier guards. Two of the night "orderlies" I never saw again!

CHAPTER NINE

TET

Fat meat, salted onions and Red parallels,
Bamboo poles, firecrackers, and green rice cakes.

—*Old Vietnamese Saying*

The Chinese new-year holiday occurred several days after my arrival. In a way, this was nice because after my initial shock of caring for war casualties and the terrific work load of catching up on some elective surgery, plus numerous casualties from recent Vietcong activity in the neighborhood, we had been busy. With the approach of Tet and the several holidays accompanying, activities slowed down. Even the VC took a rest.

One of the first things we noted was the increased number of discharges from the hospital.

The second thing was the general disappearance of many of the workers, our housekeepers, aides, and orderlies from all around the hospital area.

Whenever I tried to find out about Tet, the main answer was that it was the Chinese New Year and, as applied to Vietnam, the Vietnamese New Year. The long-term Americans said it was a combination of New Year, Christmas, Easter, the Fourth of July, and Labor Day celebrations in the United States rolled into one. (I could hardly wait to experience that!)

Later I found out that the Vietnamese calendar has a lunar cycle of eleven years that repeat every so often, and each year is named for a different animal and has a different meaning or predictable fortune for the year ahead. It was all based on ancient Chinese mythology. 1967 was the Year of the Ram. (I later learned I was born in the Year of the Tiger!)

The Vietnamese transformed it into a distinct national holiday that included family reunions, a renewing of the yearly cycle, a time of "good times," merriment, and fun. They all quit working ("quit fighting") and spent several days of eating, drinking, visiting, giving gifts, etc.

Philosophically, people were supposed to be examining their lives, assessing past deeds, seeking forgiveness for wrongs, and planning for the future. There was much visiting of pagodas (and churches), making contributions, giving to beggars, and generally being charitable with everyone, including their enemies.

During this time, they paid tribute to their past heroes and consulted fortune tellers to determine the future.

Tet officially began during the night of the next to the last night of the end of the twelfth lunar month. But initially, everyone had been getting ready for some time before, because everything closed down for several days of the holiday weekend.

As this was to be Don H.'s last night and firecrackers are a big part of the celebrating, he bought oodles of them and after sunset, we set off fireworks along with thousands of others! It sounded like a regular war! Many of the soldiers in various parts of the surrounding countryside fired their weapons in the air. Those units with machine-gun-like weapons with tracers opened up across the bay and toward the gulf. (There wasn't supposed to be anyone out there, except maybe VC and if they got hurt, who cared?) There would be bursts of tracer fire and pistol flares. In addition, there were the civilians' Roman candles and sky rockets. All rather spectacular!

It seemed as if exploding firecrackers were supposed to chase away evil spirits from the end of the past year and the beginning of the new year! Also, noise seemed to be equivalent to having a good time.

The next three days, we saw three patients (two children and an adult) who had been struck by spent bullets and who required minor surgical procedures to extract them from their soft tissues of scalp, back, and arms.

The afternoon before, I had been rambling around the hospital compound getting familiar with the place, when I saw big smoke columns boiling up into the air from the other side of town. I walked as fast as possible to the other side of the river to see and joined the maddening crowd. In some ways, it was like a comedy movie: half the people pushing toward the fire to see what was going on and the other half trying to get away. Also, there were several bucket brigades stretched out in the river passing water buckets. (No fire trucks, of course.) The fire was badly out of control, fanned by the late evening breeze. The dried-grass houses, as expected, went up like dried grass! Finally, a hose was gotten in through the crowd, along with a couple of water trucks, but the stream was less than a home-garden hose. It was pitiful. The confusion was unbelievable. Milling masses of people are the rule everywhere in Asia anyhow, but this was out of this world, unbelievable.

I even saw some Vietnamese crying, an emotion they rarely show. In fact, the only emotion I could ever get was a bland smile.

Two or three city blocks were finally leveled by nightfall, before the fire basically burned itself out.

I ran into a number of army, navy, and air force personnel, out investigating whether this was a Vietcong incident or not. Evidently it wasn't, and some days later I heard that it was caused by firecrackers that were part of the Tet celebration.

That would have really been some news back home if three city blocks of some town had been burned to the ground by fireworks during a July Fourth celebration, and there had been no fire-fighting equipment available! But here in Rach Gia, Kien Giang Province, Republic of South Vietnam, in 1967, after twenty-five or more years of war, nobody even thought of it a week later!

Our Day of Tet was notable or not notable for several events. We missed breakfast in order to get Lieutenant Commander Don H. out to the Long Strip where a navy light twin landed and took him off on his trip home. This left me as "the surgeon."

During the day, there were several radio messages and telephone relays regarding the incoming "New Team": seems as if they weren't leaving CONUS until the seventeenth, and we would be badly hamstrung for two weeks if such were the case. Later it evolved that that message referred to someone else, and our team was already in-country and would leave Saigon next week. Still later in the day, we found out they were in briefings as close as Can Tho and would be here in a couple of days, as soon as air transportation was arranged.

(I fully expected them to arrive that night in a taxi! I was beginning to be surprised by nothing.)

Before dinner, I learned how to make a Vietnamese martini: we had run out of dry vermouth, so for the base we used a half jigger of Scotch to four parts of gin and lots of ice! (Later we learned how to make "Nook Mi-tinis." This is where *nuoc mam* replaces the vermouth in the martini.)

That night, I had my first solo civilian-type surgical experience. A local family brought in their young teenage daughter with two weeks of abdominal pain. I was without my interpreters (they'd taken off for Tet), and I had to conduct my examination with a combination of sign language and examination, and I determined she seemed to have peritonitis—probably a ruptured appendix. Then I had to round up a crew (makeshift), and we operated in the middle of the night. Unbelievable: a six-foot, white Westerner removing the ruptured appendix of a Chinese teenage girl in a crumbling, run-down, foreign hospital in the dead of night in a country 12,000 miles from home, assisted by a half dozen, five-foot Vietnamese, none of us speaking the same language and communicating only by pointing and grimacing! Absolutely unbelievable!

But then Tet was only the beginning of an unbelievable and unforgettable experience!

CHAPTER TEN

THE REFRIGERATOR TEAM

Fly on a sticky field of rice and beans,
Ant strolling on a plate of beef.

—*Old Vietnamese Saying*

MONDAY 6 FEBRUARY (FOOD)

Up at 7:30. Breakfasted on one egg and small piece of toast and coffee; then over to the surgery. After a couple of cases, I made the rounds on the previous day's operative cases and checked on the more seriously ill who were still hospitalized. Then I went back to the house for lunch, consisting of the inevitable soup, canned meat, made-up sandwiches, tea, and always bananas. Afterward, I read a while, made rounds, wandered around the hospital compound, familiarizing myself with it, and waited for the inevitable call from surgery.

Things were slow as Tet approached. There were many discharges, as no one wishes to be in the hospital for Tet.

At supper, there was fried fish, a fresh vegetable salad (local grown), soup (always), butter beans, beets, wormy bread, tea, and bananas (always).

The Vietnamese household help prepared all our food. They shopped in the local markets downtown to get fresh foods, especially fruits, vegetables, and fish. Our supply officer contributed canned goods and supplies, such as sugar, tea, etc. The food was then prepared for us at the house over one or two cook stoves, such as used by the military in the field.

Believe it or not, the names of the help were Olive Oil, Betty Crocker, Bendix, and Westinghouse. Their Vietnamese names no one knew and didn't seem to count. One or a combination of the four were always around the Bac Si house, except very, very late at night, from two to four A.M. They made our beds, swept the house, washed clothes, kept the yard, cooked the food, and made various purchases. They did their shopping in the local markets (ugh!) and bought items such as bananas, fish, beans, etc. The bread was baked locally, and one had to hold it up to the light to pinch the weavil bugs out of each slice! (They were cooked dead of course, but aesthetically I couldn't deliberately eat them!) The weavils got into the flour from which the bread was made, and there was no way to get them out.

Much of the lettuce, cucumbers, tomatoes, etc., came from a lovely little garden outside our house next to the canal. It was really quite beautiful, but I was always afraid to ask about the fertilizer (knowing the Orientals' great use of night soil!)

At the table, the Vietnamese always kept a bottle of *Nuoc Mam*. This was a pungent fish sauce the Vietnamese used to dip foods into or to splash on their daily rice. It was pronounced "Nook Mahm" and was a ferocious assault on the nostrils. It had the smell of decayed fish or a fertilizer factory on a hot, damp day.

The basic foodstuffs were navy stores from the MACV storerooms.

Soup was served at every meal and the conglomeration that Olive Oil and Betty Crocker could come up with was amazing!

Bananas were the dessert at every meal—even if there was something else.

There was no milk at all, or milk products, except cheese (from the American Naval Stores).

We ate at 8, 12 noon, and 6 P.M. in our dining room in the officers' (or doctors') quarters—called the Bac Si House. "Bac Si" means doctor, i.e., Western type physician, and is probably among the most highly respected persons in their scheme of things.

There was always beer in the refrigerator, but Cokes were at a premium, and apparently the Vietnamese never heard of any of the other dozen American soft drinks. There was also plenty of gin and vodka, and some whiskey, mostly scotch, on our shelves.

The liquor was for the passers-by, for we always had people dropping in, day or night: the military types from the MAAG team across town; the FAC pilots; the "Junkies" (naval advisors on the Delta junk fleet whose base was just across the river from the hospital). They sailed the Junks—small gunboats—up and down the Delta canals and rivers looking for the VC. There were always inspectors from the USAID, from Can Tho, the American Army Headquarters in Saigon, and anyone else who happened to be wandering around in this most peculiar war.

Many of these people had no medical support and came to us for medicine for their colds, aches, skin problems, injuries, etc., and we were of course always good for a couple of free drinks. In addition, the presence of several female nurses on the premises made the place seem like a bit of home.

I felt that we were fortunate in our meals. They were palatable for the most part, and occasionally some member would surprise us with a special Italian spaghetti night or American steak night—or typical Vietnamese meal night!

CHAPTER ELEVEN

QUARTERS AND HOUSEKEEPING

Empty gate, dusty:
Moss-filled path;
All quiet, no one walking by.
And yet a garden bursting with purple and red:
For whom?

—Tran Thanh-Tong

One of the more palatable things about the entire stay was where we lived. The building was cement block, with a tiled floor and shingled (tile) roof and was one and a half stories. It was located on the backside of the hospital area across from the obstetrical building and was separated by a narrow dusty road that led toward town. Someone had fashioned a sign "The Rach Gia Hilton" and hung it over the door, and I think that told a lot. The doors were screened. The building sat on a point of land where the river flowed into the gulf and after the sun went down had a decent breeze, which helped keep the mosquito population down. Although we had mosquito netting for our beds, I confess that many nights I slept in the open on my cot, as I was too tired to fix the net. Two of us occupied a room, and Joe had a private room—he was the CO, and half of his room was the administrative office.

There were two separate toilet areas, one at the front of the house and one at the back, shared by all. We had two flush toilets and two showers (and this is what made us the "Rach Gia Hilton"). We had electricity but the generator kept coming and going, and this surge and resurge gave the place an eerie appearance always of dim lights getting a little brighter and then fading.

For the most parts, the nights were dark! A redundant statement, but only to emphasize how little house lighting, street lighting, etc., there really was. One always depended on a flashlight to help one see, even walking downtown.

The housekeepers, Bendix and Westinghouse, did our laundry. I had brought only inexpensive wash-and-wear clothing and, most of the time, lived in a surgical scrub suit anyhow. The military types had fatigues, so there wasn't much of a problem.

Some of the officers had real uniforms with them, which mildewed and which they broke out on special occasions, church, Easter, Dr. Tuan's party, etc., but this was unusual.

The water for bathing was not potable, and real drinking water was unusual. We always had a chlorinated Lister Bag available and drank only that, or boiled water, or tea and coffee. (Incongruously though, on occasion, we would get ice from the local ice plant—not purified—and use it in the booze. This we called "typhoid ice.")

Bendix and Westinghouse did the hundred of other little jobs required for running a combination boarding house, hotel, and home for transient Americans!

CHAPTER TWELVE

ROUTINE LIFE AND WORK

I wake, roll open the window,
Unaware of Spring:
Two bright butterflies
Flutter, Flutter in the flowers.

—Tran Nhan-Tong

The work and routine quickly established itself. We were there to give care to the Vietnamese people, and my donation was through surgical means and use of their hospital. This implied operating and caring for patients. I really had no one to teach. There were only the two Vietnamese physicians in the entire town (and province). It certainly wasn't anything like a vacation, so work was what was left.

I got up about 6:30 or 7:00, sometimes one half to one hour later if I'd been up most of the night before. I enjoyed the early morning hours. The sunrise was about 6 A.M., and by 8 o'clock, the sun was getting high, but the heat wasn't bad and there was a clearness about the sky and things were beginning to stir. One then realized how quiet the night had been.

The help always had breakfast ready at 8 o'clock (not before, and not after 8:30!) After breakfast, I went across to the hospital to the surgery and began my scrub. The scrub room was the space between the two O.R.'s, with two large sinks and a large, open window above. This overlooked a garden surrounded by a loose wire fence of sorts. This vegetable garden was kept by the Roman Catholic Sisters.

The windows afforded us an early morning cool breeze and, during the day, allowed passersby to look in and see how things were going.

The Vietnamese personnel with whom I was in closest contact were: Mr. Day, the surgical assistant, who was a male nurse technician, as was Mr. Chieu. They were both very good technically and whizzes with their hands. They had worked for the Vietnamese in the days of the Viet Minh and for the French and now for the Americans and South Vietnamese. (I wondered which side they would be on next year!?) Mr. Tanh was the anesthetist and Mr. Hoa was the interpreter, although Day, Chieu, and Tanh spoke passable English. The two nurses, who were always scrubbed or working in the O.R. or doubling on the floors and with whom I was most closely acquainted, were Co Nguyet, a very pretty, frail, frightened creature, and Co Thu, a more outgoing, blunt individual. They could speak English fairly well, but confused most idioms.

The American personnel were the two civilian R.N. nurses under employment by USAID, Katherine C. and Beverley R., and the two navy nurses were Anne W. and Winnie C.

There were others, of course, but our contacts were less frequent and I couldn't get their names straight and, my being so transient, I just never learned all of them.

The morning's surgery was divided between the two rooms and the doctor with the biggest, longest, or potentially more difficult case got first use of the air-conditioned room. All open-abdominal and open-chest cases were done there. Then we switched back and forth in the "number two sweat box."

This generally occupied the morning. Anyhow, by 12:30 or 1

P.M. we had to leave because the supervisor closed and locked up the surgery for "siesta," which lasted until about 3 P.M. Quite sensible, of course, in an economy and way of life that was "un air-conditioned."

We found that early afternoon was a bad time to get hurt, but fortunately, the war also took a two-hour siesta and that kept injuries down!

The days were hot as blazes between eleven and twelve, averaging 116° F. in the sun.

After lunch, I usually sunned, read, wrote, or snoozed (during the siesta time). Then came hospital rounds and clinic.

The clinics were held three afternoons a week, Monday, Wednesday, and Friday, and we used a small room off the surgery suite. This had three tables, no chairs or desks, and the windows open to the outside. Two or three doctors were generally in attendance: Joe, looking after plastic reconstructive things; Bob, orthopedic, fractures; and myself, general surgery. We each had an interpreter and a nurse-type to write down orders, etc. By the time twelve people got jammed into the room, jabbering away, examining without thoughts of modesty, it was a three-ring circus! The patients' families hung in through the windows and yelled advice, asked questions, or supplied answers. It was the damnedest way to examine patients I've seen, and after two or three hours one was worn out.

From these clinics, we got our surgical elective cases for the next week or two of operating. In general surgery, it amounted to only palpable and obvious lumps and bumps about the body. Not having X-ray diagnostic facilities or internist work-ups mitigated against a lot of routine American surgery.

But then, what we lacked in elective general surgery was always more than made up for by obstetrical emergencies, trauma, and war casualties. I guess over 50 percent of all our work during those times was war casualties: fragmentation and gunshot wounds to the extremities, abdomen and chest, and amputations from land-mine injuries.

These emergencies always upset the routine, and we seemed to sometimes never have a real routine.

The cooks served supper promptly at 6 P.M. (as lunch was

likewise promptly at noon) and if you didn't make it, too bad! Raiding the kitchen as in one's home wasn't the most pleasant, as you never knew what you were really eating when it came to leftovers!

The second nicest time of the day came about 7 P.M., when, after dinner, the sun would set, dropping like a bullet, and everything would get very still and a breeze would whip up. Tropical sunsets are something to behold, and I remembered from years before in the Philippines in World War II being entranced by the sun setting over Manila Bay. Now watching it go down over Turtle Island (Teksu) in the Gulf of Siam, I dreamed back to those days.

At night inside our house, the temperature would get down to 85°, and that was cold! It always amazes me how acclimatized one can become: It took about two weeks for the diurnal variation to change; three weeks for the climate change; six weeks for my gastrointestinal tract to straighten out; and culturally, never, I guess.

Anyhow, in the evening, we could make some hospital rounds (they had some poor lighting, and everyone wanted to get under their mosquito netting), so there weren't many patients around after darkness set in.

We wrote letters, read, played cards, drank, or sat and talked and entertained the innumerable guests who were forever passing through.

The nights invariably brought one or more emergency surgical cases. The reason was that many people coming in from VC country had spent the day hiding in the paddies or the jungle, waiting until dark to get into town without being seen. Of course, always the war went on around us. Very few days passed that we did not hear the sounds of air strikes or artillery near by.

The routine was broken by these emergency cases, by visitors coming in who needed to be toured around, by the celebration party or dinner or going away of one of the members of the team or some important person, or by the arrival of someone else back from R & R or just joining the team. Then there was the occasional trip out of town to Can Tho or a Med Cap.

Between the work, the heat, the food, and the diarrhea, I lost twenty-five pounds.

CHAPTER THIRTEEN

LANGUAGE

I know you believe you understand what you think I said, but I am not sure you realize that what you heard is not what I meant.

In the relatively short time I knew I was going to be in Vietnam, I hadn't given any thought to trying to learn any of the language. One, of course, picked up a few easy words or phrases, *Cam on* (Thank You); *Cam Cho Chi—*, etc.; plus some Vietnamese slang, *Sin Loi* (excuse me), *Het Roi* (all finished), i.e., dead (plus a good bit of American military slang: zapped, The Real World, Deros, KKK, Number 10, Rough Puff, Arvin, etc., ad infinitum).

But very shortly after arrival and constantly during my tour, I learned and was always reminded of how dependent we were on interpreters.

As we made our rounds, we were always accompanied by one or two interpreters (male), generally Mr. Hoa. Some of the nurses (aides) spoke English also. The charts and records were very skimpy and when carried by one of the workers, I could get an idea of how long the patient had been in the hospital and a rough idea of their temperature, pulse, and respirations. Orders, comments, drugs, etc., were all written in Vietnamese.

We would come to the bedside, and I would ask the patient how he was doing, the interpreter would relay this, the patient would reply, and the interpreter would replay that back to me. One really had to speak just basic English, even to the interpreters, for even *they* couldn't catch all our nuances and variations. Our words that sound similar but are spelled differently and have different meanings, e.g., write-right, five-find, four-for, would-wound (i.e., to wind), pain-pane-plane, etc., just added to the confusion of having to repeat exasperatingly slowly, going through phrases, "you hurt where?" "pain here?" ("plane here," i.e., "do you hear an airplane?") brings the response they've never been up in the air and you wonder what the hell they are talking about!

All of this led to a sort of "Tarzan-English conversation" and to this day, when confronted by foreigners, I tend to lapse into "me American doc, you Chinee nurse?" speech, even though the other party speaks the king's English better than I ever shall.

The history from the patient then ended up being simple, one-word descriptive questions: "Pain? Where? How long? Vomit? Diarrhea?" "Can't breathe? Can't urinate or defecate?" The physical exam was the most important part of the proceedings, and you had only what you could see or feel. Sometimes my diagnosis would end up as "OGK" (Only God knows) or "BORK," (Buddha only really knows!).

The idea of attempting to explain the pros and cons of various forms of treatment, surgery, etc., soon became obviously ridiculous.

As time went on, I began to wonder about any of the information we were getting. To use an example, if I were to ask a patient, "Where the pain hurt him," through the interpreter, you might imagine the patient would point to it himself. But *no*, the interpreter and the patient would have a spirited little conversation, maybe two or three minutes (what were they talking about?!) and then the interpreter would say "He hurt there" (or point it out).

If I asked the patient what he thought about American help for Vietnam, the interpreter would say maybe two or three quick words, then the patient might say two or three, in quick reply, then interpreter would turn to me and say, "he say . . ." and proceed with a five-minute patriotic speech supporting the U.S.!! It is little wonder that as time went along, I got the feeling that we were getting the information the interpreters wanted us to have.

In addition, if we left the hospital compound, the interpreters somehow were always around or showed up accidentally (?) as we wandered around the shops and streets. They were always polite, self-effacing, quiet, unobtrusive, and smiling, but omnipresent and guiding.

Any attempt at the Vietnamese language was ridiculous on my part. The tonal Oriental languages are so foreign to our way of thinking about talking that one has a difficult time learning even a few words or phrases. A few years later under other circumstances, I tried learning Vietnamese—a tough job for someone who sings every song on one or two notes!

Writing orders was no problem, as we were provided with a

57

printed checklist and learned that item one was strong-pain medicine, e.g., morphine, item number two weak-pain medicine, e.g., aspirin, etc. We just checked the one we wanted the patient to get, but the nurse gave what they wanted to anyhow, so it really didn't make any difference!

I learned about this from Mr. Ut in the famous penicillin rhubarb.

CHAPTER FOURTEEN

THE FAMOUS PENICILLIN RHUBARB

There's nothing shameful about getting out of an elephant's way.

—*Vietnamese Proverb*

One day on rounds, I was checking on a patient, an old man who had been particularly toxic from the septic effects of a large neglected abscess of his thigh, with a surrounding cellulitis. I had incised and drained this and placed him on penicillin, or rather ordered penicillin (generally available). I was looking at the chart where the nurses had dutifully noted every four hours around the clock the injection administration of the penicillin. There were about a dozen and a half little squares on the drug sheet so marked. I asked the patient casually about the shots, thinking that probably his poor, skinny frame was getting pretty sore and since his temperature was normal, we could switch to oral medication. The patient said he wasn't getting any medication or any shots. I thought perhaps there was some language communication problem, so I carefully rephrased my questions and got the answer: he really had not received a single injection in the three days!

(All of a sudden, a bell inside my head went "Ding Dong," and my mind flashed back to the second day of my arrival in country when walking around Saigon trying to figure out what was what, we had run into Foster Marshall. Foster was a very articulate orthopedic surgeon from Columbia, South Carolina, and he had led us around town for a few hours, telling us of his experiences. He had said, "I am going to tell you a story and you won't believe it until it happens to you, but sometime during your tour a similar experience will happen to you." Foster proceeded to tell us a tale that for all practical purposes duplicated what was happening to me at that moment!)

Anyhow, I sort of exploded and demanded of the nurse that if the patient had actually not received the penicillin, why had they been recording it as given on the chart?

The answer was, "Because you order it, doctor."

Now that was some kind of upside-down logic that totally escaped me, then and always, but the Vietnamese around me seemed to be on the side of the nurses, so I figured I must be dumb! There wasn't any use to complain to anyone—there was no one—no head nurse, no supervisor, no administrator. I hadn't seen Dr. Tuan for a week; neither had anyone else—what could you do?

As this was going on, the remainder of Foster Marshall's story crowded back. I asked if they hadn't given the penicillin (even though they marked down they had)! Then why not? The reply was that the hospital was out of penicillin!

"Out of penicillin" I exploded, "I don't believe it." And I didn't. They suddenly all seemed to be in complete agreement (Mr. Thanh the interpreter, Co Thu the nurse, Co Nygen another nurse, one of the Sisters and a couple of other Vietnamese) that "Yes, there is no penicillin!"

I demanded to see the pharmacist and stormed off the ward, followed by my entourage, now including some children and patients. I cut through several wards toward the front of the hospital compound and finally arrived at the pharmacy where I pounded on the door, and Mr. Ut the pharmacist smilingly appeared. I was simmered down some by then, so I could explain the situation. Mr. Ut spoke some (adequate?—one never really knew) English, and he very quietly and calmly listened and politely told me it was true. "No more penicillin in the hospital."

The bells were still ringing in my head, and I (quite boldly for me, a stranger and guest in this weird land) quickly and forcefully pushed open the half door between the anteroom and the storeroom where Mr. Ut was standing. I almost knocked him down as I strode in, looked around as he wrung his hands. Lo and behold! On one wall, there must have been a 1000 vials of penicillin! They were all neatly stacked in their little boxes: 10 cc vials of Crysticillin 500,000 u per cc—a whole wall full of shelves! I was flabbergasted. In ungentlemanly English, I cried, "What in the hell is all that for?"

Mr. Ut never lost his composure. His face was bland, smiling and unblinking, as he replied "Oh, that is for emergencies!!"

Four days later, we had penicillin again on the wards, and Mr. Ut carefully showed me the carton containing about a hundred vials of the just-received shipment from Saigon. I truly believe he wouldn't have given a single dose of the penicillin on his shelves to his own mother if she had been dying of a streptococcal infection, the one bacteria around the world that hasn't developed resistance to penicillin and even inadequate doses will kill it!

You just wouldn't believe it.

CHAPTER FIFTEEN

MR. DAY'S SIESTA TIME

They say, quick, take what Heaven has left.
Heaven's asleep and he drops things.
But work fast: when he wakes up
You'll all be dead.

—Tran Te Xuong

Really, you just wouldn't believe it. If Mr. Ut wouldn't save his mother, then Mr. Day wouldn't change his ways to save his own wife, I truly believe.

It came about this way.

We had been up all night operating. I don't know what the other members of the team had been doing, but there had been a

60

party going on, and I'd had to leave that. We had several cases, and it had been a long night and into the morning, so we just kept going with the elective schedule after a quick bite of breakfast.

By about noontime, we'd finished the cases. It was hot, my head was groggy, and I was hungry.

At that point, Dr. Tuan came in and said he had an emergency case for me, a cesarean section. Of course, I sort of wondered what the problem was, not being accustomed to merely being told to do the operation. I didn't know exactly how to go about finding out about the patient without offending Dr. Tuan. I didn't want to give the impression that I didn't believe him or didn't trust his judgment, but on the other hand, I did want to examine the patient. I asked what was the trouble, and he responded "placenta praevia, she bleed very, very much, need C-section." With that, he turned and left the surgical anteroom. He had no sooner gone than they rolled a stretcher in with a fully clothed, pale, obviously pregnant Vietnamese woman lying in a pool of blood!

I turned to find either the chief technician (Mr. Day), or a nurse or someone. They were all closing the doors, putting on their civilian clothes, obviously in the process of getting ready to leave the surgery.

As Mr. Day came up, I said, "Mr. Day, I think this lady will need surgery. I'd like to examine her, and I'll let you know."

Without breaking stride or hesitating, his reply was, "Siesta time, Bac Si, we go!" The nurses and technicians, without even looking or wondering, were heading out of the only door of the building, and Mr. Day was getting out his set of keys. While I looked dumb and stumbled around, he inserted it into the lock. Without even changing expression (the constant bland smile), he said again, "It siesta time, Bac Si, we go—NOW!!"

I scooted through the door.

He quickly and firmly closed it, locked it, and turned to walk away. All the others had gone.

I guess the consternation and amazement showed on my face and body. I tried to impress him that the patient was bleeding to death, and she surely would, in the next three hours. He merely walked on off.

I was flabbergasted, to say the least. I wanted to find Dr. Tuan to complain, to register a complaint with the Sister Superior. But they were nowhere to be found; in fact, one couldn't find much of anybody around. I finally stomped back to our quarters, intending to find consolation in griping to some of the Americans about the dumb Vietnamese. I comforted myself with our oft-quoted observation that these people were like children: they couldn't see two feet or two minutes in front of themselves! The only person around was Bendix, and he was washing clothes in the back shower.

I lay down, read Robert Ardrey's *African Genesis,* and cat-napped in the heat.

After a cool shower, I went back to the surgery building at three o'clock. All the people were there, waiting to get in. Their jabbering quieted down as I came up.

We walked in, and I rushed to the lady's stretcher; she was lying there, awake, cool and pale with a palpable pulse, still in a large pool of blood dripping over to the floor.

Mr. Day turned to me with a smile and said, "See, Bac Si, she lives; what you get so excited about?"

Trying to control my exasperation, I blurted back, as if it were the most horrible thing I could think of, "Mr. Day, she could've died!"

With his unchanging bland smile, he calmly looked back at me and said "Bac Si, we all die, someday."

CHAPTER SIXTEEN

THE VIETNAMESE (PATIENTS)

Scholar ranks first, then comes the peasant
But, when rice runs out and you run wildly about
The peasant comes first, and the scholar second.

—*Popular Vietnamese Saying*

"These people tolerate pain amazingly," I wrote in my diary on February fifteenth. The best they can hope for is a little Demerol for the most serious injuries, aspirin for fever, paraffin oil for laxative, and Dakin solution (of World War I) for neglected wounds. No tranquilizers, no salves, no ointments, potions, lotions, powders or pills. I wrote my druggist friends Fred and Mac back home that they would surely go broke in this land!

The people depended upon time, nature, and natural-body defenses for most of their cures.

All the belly cases were contaminated with dirt, feces and/or peritonitis; the soft tissue injuries were hours or days old, smelly, stinking, rotten, dirty, but somehow, after days, they got better. It was a tribute to bed rest, cleanliness, and a decent amount of food. Everyone had anemia and worms of all sorts. When I performed a laparotomy for a gunshot wound of the belly, worms were usually crawling out of the intestinal perforations!

One day, we had a call that a man was "bleeding to death" from a finger amputation. In the emergency room, I found this seventy-year-old peasant rice farmer, who lived some twenty kilometers away, indeed was bleeding from an amputation of his left finger, but not likely to bleed to death! I controlled it and repaired the stump. In the course of doing this under local anesthesia, I found out that the man had been bitten by a poisonous snake on his fingertip and, quick as a whistle, this old farmer had whipped out his machete knife and whacked off his finger to prevent the poison from spreading! He then started walking to Kien Giang (the hospital), stopping along the way to get a shot of antivenom from a local Vietnamese aide-man (whoever that was). The snake was not a cobra, but most likely a krait by the old man's story.

The ability to tolerate pain uncomplainingly was a thing that constantly amazed me. One casualty load brought an old lady in with a through-and-through body (thoraco-abdominal) gunshot wound, right chest to left chest. She had traveled only twenty-five miles from the village where she had been "accidentally" shot in night fighting between the VC and the RF-PF, but it had taken two nights and two days to get her to the hospital by sampan and cyclo bus. She had omentum hanging out of her left chest wound and at surgery had a lacerated liver, large intestine, stomach and spleen. She survived three hours of operating, without blood, received only penicillin postoperatively, and left the hospital three weeks later with a colostomy, some drains still in, and a poor, healing wound with big retention sutures in!

This was something else unbelievable in that unbelievable world! When the patients or their families decided to go home, they left. Whether you wanted them to do so or not, whether you advised for or against, argued, threatened, or predicted dire results, even death. When they were ready to go, they simply left. The nurses and techs had a delightful phrase for this "Bac Si, the patient, she escape!" I thought that perhaps there was more truth in that than the misuse of English language.

The Vietnamese believe they must die on their home grounds or territory, else the soul spends eternity trying to find its way back, a very trying experience for the individual and his family. (This also had interesting ramifications in the Vietcong's methods of killing, beheading, cutting off of hands, genitalia, etc.) Therefore, if the patient or his family felt that death was relatively imminent, out (i.e., home) they would go and the next morning we would find out about the latest escape! They went out carried on stretchers with tubes and I.V.'s running. They went out in body casts, hip spicas, and airplane splints. They even carried out a patient in a balanced traction suspension device!

It never seemed as if they blamed the hospital or doctor for what was going on. They were really rather mature and sophisticated to recognize that there is a limit as to what can be done to and for the human body to preserve a living being (not just a body that lives). They were willing to put up with science etc., to a point, but after a while, Buddha and the soul had better be appeased!

The children were as stoical as their parents: a twelve-year-old with one leg blown off below the knee and the other having an open femoral shaft fracture—lying quietly on the stretcher as we applied a splint and tourniquet. An eight-year-old with total body burns, not whimpering as we bandaged her, and another with massive, third-degree burns who mercifully died after forty-eight hours without a whimper—and no family.

We depended upon the families to look after the patients.

64

There simply were too many patients and not enough nurses of any description. The family shooed the flies and mosquitoes away, bathed the patient, turned or sat them up, fed them water or rice, soup, helped them with the urinals and bed pans, and generally looked after them. They made up the beds, cleaned the floors, and performed the other housekeeping chores. Sometimes the family would be four or five persons camping in and around the hospital grounds, sleeping alongside or under the patient's bed at night, and staying around until the patient was well enough to leave or until they decided it was time to leave as mentioned before.

Also, the families participated in treatment in an unbelievable way. If they thought the patient needed certain medicines and found out from the nurses these weren't being given, then the family would go to a pharmacy downtown and buy whatever they felt was needed, come back and administer it to the patient! They were great believers in streptomycin (50 percent of the South Vietnamese population at this time was estimated to have tuberculosis) and, on numerous occasions, I found that my patients were receiving penicillin (for example) from the hospital and a combination of penicillin and streptomycin was being surreptiously given at night by the family, along with maybe vitamins and anything else they thought was helpful. (Sure would save on drug bills for the hospital!!!)

CHAPTER SEVENTEEN

DRAMATIS PERSONAE

THE OLD TEAM

The team leader, Commander John LeB., was a U.S. Navy reservist and had been an orthopedic surgeon in Baltimore before coming to active duty. He looked like Ezio Pinza, was born in France, raised in England, and spoke with an Oxford accent. He did the trauma and orthopedic work and was the team leader on my arrival, but was finishing his year's duty tour. He was forty-five, gray bearded, pipe smoking, with a wonderful sense of humor. He had been an RAF pilot in World War II and emigrated to the U.S. because of British socialized medicine.

Major Don H., U.S. Air Force, from Ohio. He was the red-haired general surgeon who left at Tet.

Captain Bill Irish, USAF male nurse anesthetist. He was my roommate for a few days after arrival, but soon left as his year's tour was up.

Chief Petty Officer Bill T., forty years old, an eighteen-year navy man, Alabama born with Southern upbringing. He was a typical naval CPO who had been everywhere and done everything! He was an amateur authority on the U.S. Navy, cooking, the Vietnamese language, Asian seaports, fishing, scuba diving, antiques, guns, pearls, jade and precious stones—you name it—and he had a real grasp of it: music, opera, etc. He was the lab technician and an parasitologist. His duties included running the mess, supervising and looking after food purchases, and running the household. He knew every bawdyhouse in town, all the American personnel, and the gossip on them and all the important Vietnamese. He really was a fascinating individual.

Anyhow, this team has been here a year, their tours of duty were up, and they were all going their separate ways back to the States for new assignments within the next two weeks. They were supposed to be replaced by a "new team." (I experienced a bit of sinking horror once or twice, wondering what would happen if the so-called New Team did not arrive or was delayed for sometime.)

THE NEW TEAM

Commander Joe O'M., USNR, the new team leader joined the Black Watch during World War II and served with the British Army until the U.S. entered. Then his mother wanted him someplace safe in the U.S. forces, so he transferred to the marines and made the Guadalcanal landing and Solomons campaign. He finished medical school in 1950 and took a plastic surgery residency. He was a recognized herpetologist and had been on Museum of Natural History expeditions to South America and Africa to catch snakes! Also, he was a volunteer physician to the Congolese white mercenary army in Africa after the Belgians were thrown out and they were fighting the Congolese black Chi Coms (the Simbas). He was in Vietnam the previous year (1966) under MEDICO traveling around, showing how to do cleft palate and hair lip repair work.

Bob R., Lieutenant Commander U.S. Navy was an orthopedic surgeon. He was a two-year "draftee-medic," having already put in a year at the naval hospital in San Diego. Thirty-five, tall, blond, German-type from Chicago. He attended Harvard College and Northwestern Medical School. He was quiet, easygoing, determined, a loner, and was single. His hobbies were antiques, Persian rugs, and collecting paintings. I felt he would be the man behind the man and the steadying influence on this team.

Lieutenant JG Jerry H., U.S. Navy, was a male nurse, a semi-career type, about thirty with two young children. Reared in the coal mining section of Northeastern Pennsylvania, he was a regular fellow, jolly-fat-man type. He was saddled with the supply and mess duties, for which he was totally unprepared and unqualified. He also was the team's anesthetist, as he said, in his spare time!

HC3 Dennis R., U.S. Navy, the "kid" of the outfit, was about twenty years old. He was a three-year navy draftee, corpsman, lab tech, big blond farmer from the cornfields of Iowa. He had one year of college and constantly talked about girls! He manfully tried to fill the shoes left by the Chief Petty Officer.

Two navy nurses, Winnie C. and Anne W., both Lieutenant Commanders, late thirties, both single, were many-year navy nurse types, hard working, but frustrated by the terrible nursing situation here, which they can do so little to remedy. The two civilian nurses hired by the USAID (State Department) were Katherine C., R.N., and Beverley R., R.N. They had an impossible task in trying to teach American nursing standards!

CHAPTER EIGHTEEN

ARRIVAL OF THE NEW TEAM— 18 FEBRUARY

Like clouds I drifted away;
Now I am home, my house this armour,
And nothing greets me but empty palaces.

Home Coming
—Tran-Quang Khai

Two days after their arrival, the new team had established themselves in their rooms (they would be here for a year), organized their mess and quarters payments, and oriented themselves.

They came in full of vim and vigor.

Their first full day, we made complete grand rounds, going over every patient. We had approximately 100 surgical hospital patients and it seemed as if most were *mine* by that time. There was lots of work to do, especially in terms of chronic wounds, secondary closures, plastic repair, etc.

The new team tackled the Bac Si House vigorously—it was getting sort of shoddy, run-down, and dirty-junky. They scrubbed floors and walls, moved and straightened furniture, magazines, put some new drapes up and few touches of paint here and there. In a few days, the Rach Gia Hilton was taking on a new, improved, and sparkling look!

That night, Betty Crocker, Westinghouse, and Bendix fixed a fine-tasting, traditional Vietnamese dinner: crab and onion soup, boiled pork in onion and cucumber sauce, fried rice with egg yolks, egg roll, *nuoc mam* sauce, tea, and locust seeds for dessert. It was very tasty. We used chopsticks, and everyone really enjoyed it. The new team seemed quite "gung ho" and had a true *esprit-de-corps*.

CHAPTER NINETEEN

MEDCAP TO XEROR

... Whatever real military civic action there is in South
Vietnam is largely the product of United States
forces ... the informal civil action of an Army or Navy
medic ...

Peaceful Conflict
—Edward B. Glick

I rolled out at seven and dressed. Renander lent me a set of navy
fatigues, together with a hat, combat boots, and a canteen. O'Malley
let me have his .38 caliber pistol for a sidearm and the use of his
camera. My medical bag was furnished by the hospital and stocked
with "goodies" from the doctors and druggist at home. I furnished
the body to put them all together.

We stopped by and picked up the nurses, went to the BOQ
for Lieutenant (USN) Skilkett, and then drove to the navy junk base
downtown.

About 8:30 we shoved off aboard an old French river gun boat.
This was a forty-five-foot craft armed with 20-mm and 50-caliber
guns. The crew was an American navy lieutenant and four Vietnamese sailors all armed with carbines. The diesel engine putt-
putting took us out the channel into the Gulf of Siam and it was
good to smell the clean, cool, salt air and get away from the heavy,
musty, land, hot smell and feel. After some minutes we turned
down a canal and a few more miles brought us to the Junk Fleet
Outpost base at a hamlet called Xeror in the upper reaches of the
U Minh forest.

Here an approximately twenty-man U.S. Navy Force serving
with Vietnamese Navy staffed an outpost looking like something out
of a Beau Geste movie except it was sitting on the banks of a canal
in the jungle instead of in the desert.

We pulled up to a broken-down wharf between a couple of
partially submerged boats. We were helped ashore amid much talking and Vietnamese chatter. Major Bowman, U.S. Army, the local
area advisor, met us with his Vietnamese counterpart.

We walked past some crumbling buildings surrounded with barbed wire (the navy compound) and up a narrow trail-like street that quickly turned into the main (and only) street of the village. It looked like something from *Gunsmoke* or a 1930's American cowboy western movie. A few people were about the streets and lots of kids, all of whom immediately tagged along with us. They were especially attracted to the two nurses looking very uncomfortable in their fatigues and walking awkwardly in their combat boots! At the far end of the street, we came upon the little dispensary and set up shop.

At 10:30, the morning was already fiercely hot. We were sweat-soaked, and I felt tired before I even started. The word had been passed for the prior two days that the American doctor (Bac Si My) would be there today, so we had about two dozen waiting and perhaps that many more came in before everyone quit for lunch.

There were children with bad colds, coughs, skin conditions; old people with coughs, complaints of fatigue and weakness; and a few younger-type women with the same complaints. There were no men of the age range between twelve or fifteen up to fifty or sixty. One young woman had a goiter and one a breast abscess, and we tried to get them to go to the hospital, but I never did see them later, so I don't know what happened. It had taken us one and one-half hours to get here by excellent personal transportation and probably would take these people two or three days to get to Rach Gia.

At lunch, we walked back to the American-Vietnamese navy military compound and had lunch. It was strictly Vietnamese, with little bowls of rice, chopsticks, and other kinds of cooked meat and vegetables all mixed together.

Major Bowman and his boys and the Vietnamese bantered good-naturedly with each other and with us. They had received several mortar shells last night and were wondering about tonight. These American adviser types really are out in the boondocks and live the life of their counterparts.

I ate something and drank some Kool-Aid-type juice, but couldn't really get too enthusiastic about the food, although I was hungry. But my stomach hurt, and I wondered about the local food these guys had to eat every day.

Right after lunch, the FAC pilot ("Sky King") buzzed the compound in his "Bird Dog" and by roundabout radio monitoring, it seemed that he had located a large Vietcong force about ten miles away and was alerting the local SVN sector commander and Major Bowman. The plan seemed to be evolving that they were calling out the local ARVIN infantry company as a blocking force and getting some other ARVIN to land down the coast, push the VC to get him localized, then have the SVN pull away and with "Sky King" directing from the air, call an air strike, and blow the VC to pieces. I gathered this was sort of SOP in operations.

We left them to run the war and went back to the dispensary, seeing about one hundred more people. It was mostly aspirin, vitamins, soaps, diarrhea pills, and worm medicines—so many people in two and one-half hours, I could only just run them through.

At 4:30, we had to quit, because the military didn't want us traveling on the canals at dusk. (And certainly not at night—out here, the night belonged to Charlie—the Americans and Vietnamese returned to their compounds and sat out the mortars until another sunrise.)

The village chief had come by in the morning when we first got there, and he reappeared with his entourage as we were finishing. He was a nice, smiling, old man, whom I had met several weeks before. He insisted we all go to his house where we had a kind of orange-soda drink. (It wasn't Birely's—at least, it wasn't in one of their bottles.) The village chief was a real, tough, little guy, overly friendly and loved to drink.

The most interesting, fascinating real guy was the Vietnamese *Diuy* (captain). He was lean, bean-poled, tanned like hard leather, and ramrod straight. He even sat at attention. He was quiet and unassuming, with piercing black eyes. You just felt his presence. He was the local district regular Vietnamese troop (ARVN) commander. His original family had all been killed by the Vietcong, and he had been fighting for eighteen years, ever since he was sixteen years old. Like many of the professionals, he had a high price on his head.

While we were at the dispensary during the afternoon, two things had happened. The first was that the proposed or attempted operation to trap the VC unit over on the coast had fallen through. The problems with communication to get permission from the civil authorities had fouled up somewhere along the line. The local ARVN Command had to get permission from his battalion commander, who got permission from the division commander (at Rach Gia), who had to get permission from the province chief (at Rach Gia), who had to get permission from the district chief, who had to notify and get permission from the village chief! Up one chain of command, down another, and then reverse. By the time all this had been done, too much time had passed, and the opportunity for the trap evaporated! I found out later this was also standard operating procedure. What a way to fight a war!

The second bit of excitement was the capture of a VC in the town. (Alleged at least.) He was in a small hut down the street from the dispensary. They put a little interrogative pressure on him, and he reportedly gave enough information to pass along to the troop commanders. This, plus the FAC pilot's information, had gotten the operation going originally, until the chain of decision had petered out. The prisoner was jailed in a metal cage (Con Son tiger cage) inside the navy compound. I stopped by to look in on him before leaving. He could still sit up and move around a bit, in spite of the cramped space. The worst part was the blazing sun beating down on the tin roof.

These people fighting the war here at this level had no sympathy for the enemy when seen face-to-face. They are out where the going is toughest, living in and among the Vietnamese with the Vietcong crawling everywhere. At nighttime, the VC come into the village, and the military retreat within their fortress compound and sit out the mortaring that they occasionally get.

Before leaving, I checked the ARVN sailor who had been wounded in the mortaring last night. He had minor multiple frag wounds and as he wasn't going to be sent to the hospital, I made certain they gave him his tetanus shot and penicillin tablets.

About five-thirty, we got back in our little boat and started home. The ARVN sailors kept the trip interesting by firing their carbines, the .50-caliber machine gun, and the .20-mm rifle. There was no thought or concern that there might be people in the shoreline. The crew's explanation was, "All VC there anyhow!"

A couple of hours later, we got home. Jerry had come back from a long trip via plane to Saigon with fresh supplies, so there would be no more fish and rice and we could eat again.

I was awfully tired, but had two emergency operations and much good mail from home.

A very busy and interesting day!

CHAPTER TWENTY

BA MUOI BA—HUONG PHAP'S

Tea, wine and women:
My three perpetual plagues.
I must forebear.
I might be able to give up tea, maybe,
and even wine.

—Tran Te Xuong

A week or two after the entire "new team" had arrived and was established "in country," it was time for Chief Bill T. to leave. He had extended his tour of one year for six months, and this was now up. He was the last contact with the events of the year before and so was a storehouse of information.

We asked him how we could best celebrate his leaving, and his immediate and only answer was, "Dinner at the Navy Club."

Huong Phap's was six or seven blocks away in the middle of town toward the main market. This placed it relatively close to the waterfront and one of the junk fleet landing sites. I guess because the Vietnamese navy types were there originally, as time went by, the American Navy advisers began using it as their gathering place when they came in off the Gulf from their Swift Boat patrols. It was only natural that any other old navy salt in the area would sooner or later find out about this place and seek out the companionship of his own service types. Chief Bill spoke often of Huong Phap's—the Navy Club—and we looked forward to this nightclub, restaurant, entertainment area, "Vietnamese USO," et cetera, all rolled into one!

I was busy during the morning and did another child tracheostomy for diphtheritic croup obstruction. There was reported to be an outbreak of diphtheria in the province between us and Can Tho, and the evening before I'd done a "trach" on a moribund, one-year-old girl who died. The mother brought the child in, in her arms—absolutely blue-black—cyanotic from obstruction of the pharynx and upper airway, and the tracheostomy was done practically with the mother holding the child, but was too late.

Part of the morning was spent trying to figure out how to discharge or get rid of some of the patients. On one ward, I had fourteen beds but twenty-one patients! Unbelievable!

Betty Crocker gave us a light lunch of some kind of Vietnamese shrimp soup. We complained of not enough to eat and being hungry. She just laughingly apologized, "Ten thousand Cambodian *Sin Lois*" (i.e., a thousand pardons)! Nighttime you go Huong Phaps."

Siesta time was interrupted by the arrival in the E.R. of four Rough Puff (the Regional Forces—Popular Forces), soldiers with twenty-four-hour-old injuries. They had all been injured by a land mine in the Kein Luong district about fifty kilometers away the day before and had spent the night in a neighboring hamlet, waiting for daylight to get transportation to come to the hospital. Three of the cases we debrided and dressed under local in the E.R. and admitted. The other case we had to take to the O.R. for Bob to attempt to salvage his foot and leg.

It was late when we got through, and I was starved. We hitched a ride over and joined the rest.

Huong Phap's was a rectangular, two-story building set back from the street with a courtyard centrally, and this opened to the street through two separate gates—or the remains of gates. There were tables scattered about, and lines of light bulbs were strung overhead to give a light of sorts. A few of the bulbs were yellow, blue, and red, so it gave a very eerie effect. There was music coming from somewhere: sometimes in Vietnamese (or Chinese), and sometimes in English.

Everyone was drinking beer—the local French-Vietnamese beer 33—*Ba Muoi Ba*. When spoken quickly running it all together, the word was "Bahmebah." This came to mean any kind of non-American, beerlike drink. Formaldehyde was used as a preservative, giving it a phenol-like taste and a hell of a headache for a hangover!

You wouldn't get your glass half empty before some little girl was pouring it full again.

Chief Bill was in his glory, the perfect host, everywhere shaking hands, slapping backs, and cracking jokes, even with the Vietnamese who didn't really appreciate or cotton to touching as a friendly, familiar gesture.

We sat at the long wooden tables on long benches. The tables were covered with checkered tablecloths that I guess were clean, although they had that tired, tattletale-gray look to them. The napkins, however, looked dirty. In front of you was a little bowl and a pair of chopsticks.

The food was set on the table, passed around, and one helped oneself. Eventually, everything ended up all mixed up in the bowl, or portions thereof.

First, we had some sort of shrimp with rice wafers, not unlike potato chips. Then a mixture of lettuce, shrimp, and tomatoes, covered with an evil-looking, yellow sauce, from which we all knew we would get the GI trots! The Cha Gio was the best. This was a thin, rice paper pastry covering around some kind of meat—whatever the cook decided—pork, fish, etc., and deep fried. This Vietnamese version of the Chinese egg roll I found was always particularly good in South Vietnam and later times felt I could at least get *something* I could eat! Then we had the South Vietnamese variation of Chinese Won-Ton soup, which we drank from our bowls. Then the inevitable fried rice and chicken bits. *Com Tay Com* was rice cooked with a mixture of mushrooms, chicken, and ginger sauce. For dessert, there were large hunks of very sweet pineapple.

The "Bahmebah" flowed liberally during these courses.

All of this was set in the semidarkness, while we shooed flies and swatted mosquitos, with the lights fading and brightening as the town's electric current surged and regressed.

The record player had American 45 rpm records on a 33 rpm player (or vice versa) blasting as loudly as possible. Little children played around, came and stood, watching you eat and talking to each other about you as you ate, with the Vietnamese girls pouring beer as fast as you could drink it. It was an unbelievable, nightmarish, but not unpleasant experience. We lasted until midnight, then went home and Joe pulled out a bottle of brandy, which we drank to sterilize our guts!

CHAPTER TWENTY-ONE

DR. TUAN'S DINNER—25 FEBRUARY

The road was well guarded, its thousand houses stayed
Shut and silent;
Officials of all seven ranks attended in full uniform
And a white-haired soldier, too,
Who kept telling tales of Nguyen-phong.

—Tran Nhan-Tong

One day, invitations were left for us at the Bac Si house from Dr. Tuan, the Medicine Chief of the province and hospital. They were printed (how that was arranged in this God-forsaken place I didn't know) and had a formal air about them. Commander O'Malley told us that we would have to go "formal." For the military, that meant putting on a uniform instead of fatigues and for me, putting on a tie with my one sports suit instead of a scrub suit.

We were all anxiously awaiting Saturday night and this gastronomical assault on our bodies!

The day before was a busy one. It started out at dawn with a Vietcong raid on the Short Strip to try to damage the FAC planes there. We were awakened by the gunfire—it was only a mile away. I had been out there flying a day or two before. After a while, four ARVN soldiers were brought in with gunshot wounds. This kept us going into the afternoon.

During this time, an A.M.A. USAID Bac Si (like myself) from Long Xuygen came by. He was finishing his tour and was ready to return home to private solo practice in Oregon. He was very upset

Our hope for the future of Vietnam

The patient and long-suffering people of Vietnam

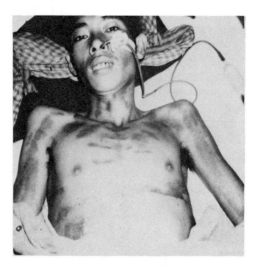

"Chinese medicine"—note the bruise marks from pinching the skin to relieve the pain of peritonitis.

Canals and fishing boats in downtown Rach Gia

Surgical technicians and interpreters and the "Rach Gia Air Force"

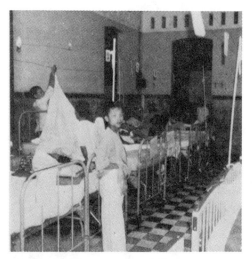

Typical surgical ward: Putting up nightly mosquito nets. Note crowded beds.

Medical auxiliary personnel technicians of the Kien Giang Province Hospital and "The Surgeon"

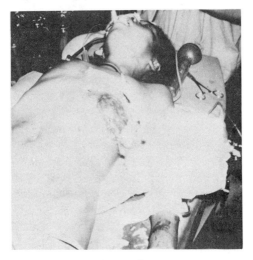

Civilian war casualty in the emergency room

and disappointed with this tour. Seems as if the Australian surgical team there didn't get along with the Vietnamese surgical team, and he didn't get much pediatric or general practice work because of the lack of cooperation. He was amazed at our work and particularly our war casualty rate, as I toured the hospital for him between and after cases.

In the evening, we went out to walk in the hospital compound to stretch our legs after the long day and, hearing strange music "noises" from the front side of the hospital, I went out across the street. In the courtyard of the Buddhist temple was a large crowd watching a traveling outdoor theater group who were putting on a performance.

The player had a garish, outlandish-appearing costume with white rice-flour face makeup, and loud disconcerting music—cymbals, sticks, bugles, and a thousand people jammed around, milling, talking, laughing, and watching.

We (three Americans) caused as much commotion as the players did. The children were running back and forth at us, pulling, tugging, begging, and making so much noise that it was embarrassing us. They seemed completely undisciplined. We finally had to leave.

Saturday arrived, and the surgical team had scheduled no elective work. The night had been quiet and we all felt good, so we made a complete tour of all the surgical patients—about 150—during the morning. It was one of the few times we were able to do this formally on everyone! At that, the four hours averaged about ninety seconds a patient, so we didn't do a lot of "Southern-Home-Folks-Gabbing" type of patient care!

That was the way it always was: too many people, too few workers, too much to do. You could start off fresh Monday morning with elective operations; emergencies in the afternoon and night; repeat it Tuesday and by Wednesday, you couldn't remember what you'd done first on Monday!

Although Dr. Tuan's home was only four blocks away from the hospital, we all rode together in the Scout, so as to be as relatively fresh and free from dust and sweat as possible when we arrived.

The party was to honor the new surgical team, and all the big-shot civilians and military of Kien Giang province and Rach Gia were there.

81

It would be like having the governor of North Carolina (the province president), the province chief (a military man, who is the real power), the mayor, police chief, the two doctors, a couple of International Red Cross bigwigs from Geneva who were looking over the hospital setup, plus numerous other dignitaries of the town and province.

I understood this party was somewhat unusual, as the last team was not so honored.

There was much booze of all sorts (including American Bourbon), and everyone was tanked. Then we had a stand-up meal around little tables—Oh, my GI tract again! But we have to be political and social—win friends and influence people—our job as much as taking care of people. One of the delicacies I found at this meal was *Chao Tom*: this was a shrimp paste, rolled around a sugarcane stick, and boiled. It went well with whiskey.

I didn't have any brilliant discussions of anything with anyone. Most of the people talked to each other in Vietnamese and/or French. We few Americans wandered in and out, trying to look interested, and answering as sanely as possible. It was hot as hell, the mosquitos and bugs kept our hands and bodies moving, and the crowd and liquor kept us sweating. I could hardly wait for the food to begin to work on my innards.

One of the interesting conversations I latched onto was with a Vietnamese businessman in town who got to telling us about *Nuoc Mam*. This sauce is to the Vietnamese what soy sauce is to the Chinese.

It seems that a town called Phan Thiet about ninety kilometers east of Saigon was the major center of production. This city of about 60,000 on the coast had more than 500 fishing boats bringing in the raw material—fish.

Traditionally, *Nuoc Mam* was made in twelve-foot-high wooden vats, bound with fiber ropes. Layers of small fish—preferably sardines—and salt are alternated in the vat on top of a charcoal filter. A little saltwater starts the fermentation, and the liquid running from the bottom of the vats is poured back time and time again. The process is supposed to take three months.

Some producers dilute it and/or make it with freshwater fish. (These are more plentiful, cheaper, and less dangerous to catch than small-boat fishing in the South China Sea or the Gulf of Siam. They are also less rich in protein.)

South Vietnamese law required that "first quality sauce" must have at least twelve grams of protein per liter of sauce.

In addition, coopers, bottle vendors, pot makers were all kept busy supplying some 200 *Nuoc Mam* factories, most of which were small-cottage industries.

About 9:30, a number of us left and went to the nurses' house where various of the American military congregated for their Saturday-night brawl. They were all thoroughly tanked by midnight.

I had to quit, so as to be able to take care of the emergency room if needed, thankful for the excuse.

CHAPTER TWENTY-TWO

FOUR DAYS IN FEBRUARY (QUOTED FROM THE DIARY)

I'll pick a snake-filled spot,
Linger in its country delights.
Sometimes, I'll climb the one tall mountain
And whistle until the sky
Turns me cold.

The Ideal Retreat
—Khong Lo

MONDAY 27 FEBRUARY #36

Up and at 'em. Long schedule today including real good case! GSW perforation of upper right calf about six weeks ago in RF/PF soldier who developed A-V fistula. Richter and I repaired the fistula and excised the false aneurysm. Also did C-section, appendectomy (they are all perforated and retrocecal) and colostomy cases. Lt. Col. Dooling USAF (thoracic surgeon from Florida) is new MOC at Can

83

Tho and he flew down for the day to view our setup. Had him see chest cases for us. I was very tired and late for supper. Had a number of brandies and sat and talked medicine with Joe and Bob for a couple of hours and then to bed early.

TUESDAY 28 FEBRUARY #37

Up early and another busy morning schedule: Jerry H. and Bob R. left this morning for Saigon to conduct team business—money, purchases, etc. and will be gone three days. Troops on Junks and Jeeps left out hell bent this morning and artillery going all morning—big doings somewhere nearby and will mean more casualties by nightfall. Among interesting cases was imperforate anus and recto vaginal fistula on two-week-old child. Lay down and napped during siesta and awoke with terrific headache which haven't been able to shake: Clinic and rounds. Their diseases are only in the advance stages: Grade IV Carcinomas of cervix; Ovarian cyst size of six-month pregnancies; goiters size of grapefruit, etc. Col. Bellinger (the local MACV CO) came by for drinks and talk. Quiet dinner and reading and writing afterward. Artillery still going tonight.

WEDNESDAY 1 MARCH #38

Writing at 1:30 A.M. Thursday morning: very busy day yesterday—or this morning rather. Operated till 11:30 and congratulating ourselves on a couple of free hours when eight V-N soldiers (RF/PF) brought in just at lunch all shot up—multiple injuries, etc. Started operating again at 12:30 and finished at 5 o'clock. Did absolutely beautiful case: a terrific shattering wound of the right humerus about one-half was approximately six inches length just blown out and pulverized and along with it the brachial artery. I went in and found the two ends and anastomosed them using 6-0 silk and bending the arm. Tonight he had a good radial pulse. Have felt crummy—headache, chills, fever, etc. all day and drank Manhattan

84

before and after supper and passed out about 9 P.M. Awakened now at 1 A.M. with lady with dead baby hanging out half way and will have to do destructive operation C-section. I am waiting for O.R. crew to get in and set up. She was sent in from the district after twelve hours' labor with eight grams HBG and no blood—Oh me! Hope the saying about the March weather—"In like a lion and out like a lamb"—holds for surgery, don't think I can keep this up.

THURSDAY 2 MARCH #39

Many letters; Joe O'M. always bellyaching about my getting so much mail! Box of furadantin from drug store, muchly appreciated and needed. Bob R. back from discouraging trip to Saigon. Jerry H. hopefully will get back tomorrow with food, gas and supplies—we are short. I still have not received my check from home to pay my bills with yet: I hope to see it soon.

In halting English over the telephone there is a voice saying "P-C-C." (in Vietnamese: *Phom Khu Khop*) This is the surgical emergency room. Whenever there was an E.R. case bigger than a simple sprain or laceration they always call and these are about the only words they can say in English. It's hopeless to try to get any information as to what the case is all about and much simpler to get up and walk over to the hospital which is only two minutes away anyhow.

At night walking through the back entrance to the hospital is an experience. One has to challenge the rats for the right of way on the sidewalks. These are big wharf rats and scurry all over the place—hiding in the grass and sewers. Joe is having the grass and shrubbery stuff cut out so as to eliminate some of their hiding places, but that is a slow process. He's forever threatening to go out with his sawed-off shotgun at night and blast them, but we are afraid he'll start a minor war if he does! Some jittery guard would probably start shooting the place up!

In addition to the rats and mosquitoes there are the lizards that are always on the floors and walls. Fantastic! The Gheko lizard has a sound like "F-K you" and are omnipresent. They are our mosquito repellents! I woke up one night with one crawling over my face! Frightening!

All the refuse and garbage that is thrown out and around plus the open sewers of course makes for all this unsanitary mess. No one seems to mind—they just throw out the Sister's rice if there is any left over.

CHAPTER TWENTY-THREE

"OH, WE HAVE MANY—"

I've always meant to ask you,
Meant to, tried to,
Started to, afraid,
Afraid, always too shy.

—Xo Xuan-Huong

One day after I'd been there a number of weeks, we were in the middle of an abdominal operation and struggling. This particular Vietnamese was big—for a "namese" (most of them were small)— and when doing an emergency laparotomy for trauma, when you cut them from Xiphoid across the umbillicus to the pubis, everything sort of lay open. It was easy to plow around in all internal areas to work on whatever was needed from the liver in the right upper quadrant to the sigmoid colon in the left lower quadrant and anything in between. Also, I always had helping me either Mr. Cheiu or Mr. Day, the two outstanding surgical technicians who were surgeons *par excellence* in their own right, with many years of experience helping Vietnamese, American, Japanese, French, and Australian surgeons. They literally could do almost anything technically—surgically—their only problem was you had to tell them what to do.

Thus, we were always able to get good exposure operating on these little people, by using our hands and holding the body cavity open as we needed.

Anyhow, this particular late morning, I guess I was getting tired and I said to Mr. Day in my best Asiatic-Pig-Latin-English, "Mr. Day, in America, we have instrument, called self-retaining retractor. It holds belly open; make operation easy."

He replied easily, "Oh, Bac Si, we have many of them. In fact, we have a number out in our warehouse."

I was astonished.

After the case, I asked to see the warehouse, and we walked across the hospital compound to a small wooden building behind the medical-ward complex. Inside, in one of the rooms, we found a shelf containing several boxes, containing one each of a Balfour self-retaining retractor packed in cosmoline.

I was amazed. Unbelievable!

I commented about us operating all these weeks without this valuable surgical instrument that I didn't know they had and they never had put them out for my use.

"You never asked for them before," was the answer!

CHAPTER TWENTY-FOUR

"YOU NEVER ASKED . . ."

> There are no guts,
> No others
> No you.
> Buddha-past
> Buddha-present
> Buddha-future,
> Are all the same.
>
> *The Essence of Buddhism*
> —Ly Thai Tong (999–1054)

One Sunday morning, I was catching up on my mail after a leisurely breakfast, enjoying the coolness of the dining area before the sun got too high. An aide from the hospital rushed in, out of breath, saying I must come quick, "Soldier, hurt."

I walked quickly toward the E.R. thinking this was another

casualty being brought in. However, the aide tugged at me and led me past the quiet E.R. surgical suite toward the front of the hospital compound to a small, low building. Part of the administrative complex, I thought. He led me into a small room, in the middle of which sat an ultra-modern dental chair in which sat a Vietnamese soldier, evidently in much pain. "See, soldier, him hurt."

Yes, I had to agree, but it hadn't been as I'd supposed!

I went up to the soldier and, getting him to open his mouth with some probing and tapping, I figured out that he must have an abscessed tooth and I was about to become a dentist!

There was a well-equipped dental table nearby, and I searched for some anesthetic and extraction forceps.

As I was doing this, I became aware for the first time that Mr. Cheiu, the O.R. Surgical technician, was sitting on a bench in one side of the room watching quietly. He had not acknowledged that anybody was there or anything was going on.

Anyhow, I got so engrossed in trying to anesthetize the soldier's gum and jaw and get the tooth pulled, I forgot about Mr. Cheiu. For twenty or twenty-five minutes, I sweated, tugged, fiddled, repositioned, pulled, cursed, jiggled, and the soldier squirmed, slid, slobbered, and sobbed until I finally got the damn tooth pulled with a feeling of great triumph and satisfaction!

After all this demonstration of physical effort (violence?) I sort of stepped back and the soldier rearranged himself in the chair.

At this instant, Mr. Cheiu lightly and expertly draped himself around the dental chair and the patient and, talking softly to the patient, picked up the dental mirror and, deftly and quickly, cleaned and packed the bleeding socket! He looked more dental than most dentists!

I was flabbergasted.

"Mr. Cheiu," I sputtered, "You knew how to do this all along. Why didn't you pull his tooth?"

Unflappable. "Bac Si, you never asked me."

Unbelievable!

CHAPTER TWENTY-FIVE

PARKINSON'S LAW OF VIETNAM GEORGE

The six knowledges obsess us at night, all night,
Darkness in our minds confuses us.
Night and day I listen to the bell, and learn,
Lose my laziness and find understanding.

Awakening
—Vien Hoc

And this I found to be a sort of truism, a sort of Vietnamese Law 33 or Parkinson's Law of Vietnamization.

If you let it happen, the Vietnamese would step back and let you do all the work. Not from the point of view of being lazy or stupid, or ornery, but from the point of view of passivity. The Americans, with the best of intentions to help or teach or show, would start in with a job, project, operation, anything large or small, many or few people or things involved. Whenever it didn't go just to the satisfaction of the Americans, they would increase their activity, their input, and thus gradually drive out the Vietnamese. Pretty soon, the Americans would be doing it all, whether it was putting out a fire in some remote hamlet, building a generating plant in Saigon, or growing crops in the highlands, or pulling a tooth in Rach Gia. We just seemed to be unable to let them do "their thing" and eventually get around to the same end result, maybe not what we would have liked exactly, but close enough.

I found this time after time in many aspects of military and medical life in 1967 and years later in 1969 and 1970. You could do things your way, but you must let them use their methods, even if you knew yours were better. One shouldn't even suggest things, because you were not there long enough to know an individual well enough to do that. One should leave the initiative for adopting our techniques strictly up to the Vietnamese.

Afterward, I coined my own phrase of "Vietnam George" whenever I experienced the situation of one person or faction gradually taking over while others would quietly and passively step aside, and first thing somebody else was doing all the work while the others were reaping up the profits!

This was Parkinson's Law of Vietnam George: "Let the Americans do it if they think they are so damn smart and we are so damn dumb."

And they did.

CHAPTER TWENTY-SIX

CAN THO RUN —9 MARCH

Puffs of wind, reeds rustle,
Birds circle, hurry, half lost in the dusk.
Loaded with wood he comes slowly home:
He knows the way and won't lose it.

A Woodcutter on His Way Home
Anonymous—Vietnam

One of the pleasures of visiting places is just that, to visit around and see what it is all about. That was why I was always eager to visit around in the hospital and meet the patients, nurses, and families; to walk in the town and get the feel of the sights, sounds, and smells; and finally to see the countryside.

This latter was rather limited because of security. One just didn't go junketing around by oneself, and the language and difficulty of travel were enough to prevent you from wandering too far afield.

However, when I got the opportunity, I was always ready to go. Thus one day it was decided that the team had need to get some supplies and to turn in items for repair. A trip to Can Tho was necessary. Can Tho, the provincial capital of Phong Dinh province, was also the largest city in the Mekong Delta area south of Saigon and was the center of all military, governmental, administrative, transportation, and supply activities for the area of South Vietnam, categorized as the Fourth Corps Area. USAID had a subheadquarters here and regional administrative offices. We had four air conditioners that didn't work and needed repairing, and the stove in the mess required butane gas, which had been out for several weeks. (Betty Crocker had been cooking our meals on three little Coleman lantern stoves, "Number Ten," she says!) Also, the mess needed some beer and Cokes and some "drug store-like" items (American type) that couldn't be got locally, so all in all there was good reason for a "run." One of the nurses needed to make a physically present report to her boss at the navy office. Jerry was the supply and mess officer and, of course, had to go. Bob wanted to go for the trip and since two vehicles would be required, two drivers were needed. Also, they wanted two "shotguns." The nurse would be one, and I volunteered for the other.

The Thursday morning rolled around, and we dressed for the dusty ride ahead, using operating room masks to cover our faces and an ARVN campaign hat. We checked our pistols, carbines, and the two small trucks rolled out of Rach Gia north to Can Tho.

The road at one time had been paved, but hadn't been repaired for ten years and consequently was terrible—rutted and potholed. It was narrow to start with, and the shoulders were run down and rough. There was a terrific amount of traffic, mostly people, cyclos, motor bikes, jeeps, occasional ARVN convoys and a rare, old French Citroen car. The bridges were all one-way and mostly had little fortlike guard towers with soldiers, who didn't really direct traffic. Whoever got there first or bluffed the most went first!

We passed through a dozen hamlets, all looking rather poor, dirty, and run down. Close to Rach Gia, there were several resettlement hamlets of the Roman Catholic North Vietnamese who had come South in 1954–55. These had a neater, more orderly appearance than the others.

About 11 o'clock, we arrived in town and drove to the USAID headquarters and reported in. They directed us to the motor pool, where we turned in the trucks to have them serviced while we were in town. We borrowed one of their jeeps to get around in and drove around town, which had a bigger, more spacious feel to it than Rach Gia.

We again visited the province hospital to see Major Frank Camp and the American Air Force Milphap team, then to the quartermaster for supplies, and then the MAC-V headquarters where we had lunch in the PX. The hamburgers, French fries, and Cokes tasted good after our weeks of rice and shrimp. Unfortunately, they had run out of ice cream, so we did without that. We picked up various drugstore items and by three o'clock, we were ready to leave.

On the way back, we went to Bien Thuy Air Force Base to check their PX for various items and then into the officers club for a drink.

Again on the road and fortified by the O-club stop, it was a hell of a wild ride back. The guys were afraid of being on the road after dark, so we slammed through villages and practically jumped the bridges.

Back in Rach Gia, I quickly showered to get the dirt and sweat off and grabbed a quick bite of late supper. They had been sitting on a mortar fragment, belly-wound case for three hours. I operated on that case and finally got back to my room late where I found much mail, including pictures from home and a big box of candy, gum, cakes, cookies, and other goodies.

I appreciated them so much and passed most of them out to the children. I taped the pictures to the wall, along with my others.

By midnight to bed, thankful for an eventful day and a safe, if strenuous trip. Someone has to make it once a month because some supplies can't be always brought in by airplane—particularly the bottled gas—and someone has to go after it. In this country, railroads had long since become inoperative because of guerrilla warfare. The highways were usable by armed convoys only, so this left a choice of airlift, oxen, or bicycles for transport!

CHAPTER TWENTY-SEVEN

DIARY EXCERPTS FROM MID-MARCH (QUOTED)

A brook runs
In the small, flat Phuc-Hung Garden.
By the plum-bower the snow is gone, blossoms begin.
With no clouds the bamboo stand is a pearl verandah.
The sun: I ask a friend for tea.
After the rain I have my herb plants re-set.

The Phuc-Hung Garden
—Tran-Quang Kha (1241–1294)

WEDNESDAY 8 MARCH

Busy schedule this A.M.—five major—afternoon orthopedic clinics and rounds. Joe O'Malley back at suppertime after big review at Bien Tuy Air Force Base. Seems a four-star general inspected and had buddy James Stewart (BGUSAF Res) along. After supper went to town to TOC to get trucks gassed for trip to Can Tho in A.M.—stopped in market and bought myself Vietnamese campaign hat to cover from dirt and heat—

FRIDAY 10 MARCH

Full morning schedule and tired after yesterday (Can Tho trip). Took nap after lunch—overcast and muggy—surgical clinic and rounds. Dr. Tuan came over before supper—been to Saigon and gotten three million more piasters (total now about six million) with which to improve hospital: New OB unit, another operating room—plans to use about three million to build himself office and clinic! Their philosophy of all for me first and the deuce with anyone else—

SATURDAY 11 MARCH

Total grand rounds this A.M. took three hours—see and dress everyone and thoroughly go over charts. Big box of goodies from home and children plus recent pictures—party for American military personnel (MAAG team) in the area. Number came in from boondocks—about 100 during evening—hit of the Rach Gia social season.

I had chills, fever, headache, all night and woke up feeling badly.

SUNDAY 12 MARCH

Managed to struggle out by nine, took some tetracycline and APCS and went to Roman Catholic Mass. Saw patients. Bob R. fixed pancakes, afternoon began writing paper on medical aspects of practice—lay in sun and sweated out my bad feeling—

MONDAY 13 MARCH

Many favorable comments on party—the COVANS (counterpart Vietnamese American—what the V-N call the American Military Advisors) have a tough lonely job here. Living in the country with the ARVN troops, eating and drinking their food, getting mortared at night and sniped at by day—all glad to get into town for a good drunk occasionally where they let their hair down and tell hair-raising tales.—I have abdominal cramps and diarrhea again today. Joe O'M. up with same.

TUESDAY 14 MARCH

—Had father-son combo injured by VC grenade. Father was a "Rough-Puff" and son going along to carry guns. VC threw grenade and father threw it back. Both had multiple wounds and required operating all afternoon and much blood, but will live—

WEDNESDAY 15 MARCH

Day started off in usual busy fashion. Australian Surgical team from Long Xuygen coming down for visit—four docs and four nurses and four E.M. all supposed to fraternize for lunch, but Big Flap at one o'clock. As they arrived we were snowed with casualties so we spent afternoon operating. At five o'clock tired and discovered gas gangrene in young patient's leg and had to do emergency above knee-amputation. Don't know what happened to the Australians—birthday party at Co Bac Si (nurses house) for Dennis R. our Iowa Country boy lab tech.—Joe O'M. and "Sky" King got into a flap over going on night flight—Joe was tanked and left. Party happier.

THURSDAY 16 MARCH

—Very tired when got up this morning and had light schedule, thankfully. Awfully hot. Complete rounds and seems as if we get further behind and overcrowded. Women's wards jammed. Again at 11 o'clock big casualty load influx—did emergency amputation for neglected mortar wound of foot, she had it and other injuries and the neglected infections requiring surgery.

The chloroquin-primaquin malaria prophylaxis kept a forty-eight-hour stomach ache going and caused a tired, dragged out feeling.

SATURDAY 18 MARCH

—Last night brought simmering discord between team and Joe to a head. Mainly between Bob and Joe. Joe called us into his room after we got into an argument over the medications we were carrying out on the Medcap. Joe said he felt antagonism, and well—there is. Bob beat around the bush and would not voice directly his opinion about Joe drinking. He did point out the incident of the other night when we were playing bridge and Beverly R. was here and Joe walked out in the nude to go to the bathroom across from the kitchen! Joe tries to play the big man, etc. and he is always "Rocks and Shoals" (a Marine Corps expression for Army's "G.I."), always talking about fighting the Simbas, or when he was in the Black Watch—or on the "Canal" (i.e. Guadalcanal), or "I've been here before, you know" (i.e., the six-week tour last year with MED-ICO). He has an overexaggerted sense of his own importance coupled with his heavy drinking and he has things frequently screwed up. Also said he got a "Dear John" letter from his wife. I wouldn't blame her—if he is at home like he is here! Anyhow we all sat down and thrashed it out and I believe the air somewhat clearer afterward—I fear for team during the next ten months if the past six weeks are any indicators.

At 7 A.M. two kids, age six and fourteen, brought in with serious gunshot wounds (VC attacked their hamlet five miles from here at 4:30 this morning) so I spent the morning patching up intestines, liver, lungs. During afternoon we had more casualties plus a ruptured appendix case. Supper of Chao Giao and rice with chopsticks. Had just gotten to bed when five RF/PF soldiers wounded in land mine explosion were brought in. Took care of them. They had been accompanied by a young American *Duiy* (Covan-My) Captain Zadnovzy—so young and all alone with these undependable jerks in the mangrove swamps. I took him to the Bac Si house and gave him ice water (boiled instead of chlorinated) and a big chunk of Jean Cornwell's pound cake and took a can of instant coffee off our shelves and gave him. (Maybe someday he will do the same for my boys . . .)

MONDAY 20 MARCH

. . . No mail for a week and at noon mail plane came in and deposited a tremendous stack. I had a dozen letters—all two weeks old—good to hear from someone again—beginning to get lonesome—another hectic busy schedule, many interruptions and lots of admissions. Jerry H. and I worked on cleft lip repair movie . . .

WEDNESDAY 22 MARCH

Did cleft lip this A.M. which we filmed in O.R. Lost patient from mesenteric thrombosis post-op. Hot. Evening I went down to market place with tape recorder—got some folk band music. Sounds like bagpipes. Had a slow day. Still having stomach troubles occasionally and still loose stools.

FRIDAY 24 MARCH

Well, as we were getting into our scrub suits this morning I said to Joe, "Guess I shouldn't 'bad mouth' us, but you know things have been sort of quiet last two or three days, as far as war casualties go." He said, "Hush," and I should have. About 10:30 we had a rush of eight people brought in—all brought from VC country and therefore presumed to be (VC)—all shot up in an air strike last night. We did four amputations plus all the other stuff—ran over into the middle of the afternoon.

CHAPTER TWENTY-EIGHT

CHINESE MEDICINE

A body is like lightning, gone in a moment, back to
Nothingness,
As spring flowers are dead in the fall
Forget about this growing and dying, it is all irrelevant.
Life's motions are like dew on the grass.

Man's Body
—Van-Hanh

We were the *Bac Si My*. This literally meant: *Bac-omniscient* and *Si-Educated* (person). (That was a pretty tall order, even for a Harvard man, I thought!) *My* meant American.

However, the major volume of medical care for the Vietnamese was carried out by the *Dong-Y* (Dong-*Oriental* and Y-*Medical*), of whom there were 10–15,000 in Vietnam. Their learning was through an apprenticeship system and with only a few months' background and training, they could open shop!

The Vietnamese were of Mongol origin and carried much Chinese culture with them (although the Chinese are their traditional enemies). Also recently (100 years), many Chinese have emigrated, and most maintain their ancient traditions. Cholon, where we had our first meal in-country, was a large suburb twin city of Saigon and was populated largely by Chinese.

So-called "Chinese medicine" was really "folk medicine." It was called Chinese in the same sense that we Americans speak English, although we are hardly very British!

In this type of folk medicine, it is believed that disease occurs according to the localization of pain and, therefore, treatment is directed to that area. The type of treatment is roughly related to the location and severity of pain, as well as success with similar treatment in the past.

This type of treatment was basically one of counterirritation, practiced by vigorously pinching the skin with the fingers or by applying suction cups. The aim was to produce bruises or marks on the skin overlying the area where the pain was located. The amount of treatment was related to the amount of pain. (The treatment of flulike symptoms involved the entire body!)

The use of this friction pinching of the skin produced vertical deep red bruises. A frequent pattern was that of lines radiating down the base of the neck out to the clavicles (sore throat).

Cupping was done by using tumblers (glasses) and heating the inside with a candle, then placing the open end down over the intended area. As the air inside cools, a suction is created that left a circular ecchymosis. It was especially used for abdominal and upper-back problems.

The people (patients) generally try folk medicine first. The *Dong-Ys* are frequently familiar with the patients, and this gives additional clues regarding disease and treatment.

The practices of pinching, cupping, moxa, acupuncture, and the use of herbs are combined with fortune-telling, superstition, and astrology in the entire spectrum of "Chinese Folk Medicine."

I saw many patients with these marks over all portions of their body during my stay there and when operating on all sorts of conditions.

One of the most amazing (fantastic) events was that involving a "Rough Puff" local soldier who was shot in the abdomen. I operated and found he had penetrating wounds of the small and large intestines, with anticipated fecal peritoneal contamination. He developed a generalized peritonitis and was quite toxic. By the fifth postoperative day, he was raving and irrational, highly febrile, vomiting around the nasogastric tube with a greatly distended abdomen. At this time, I had some Chloromycetin from home and started it intravenously. But that night, the family was getting upset and fidgety, and they called in the Chinese-medicine doctor (without our knowledge). The next morning when I went by to see him, his body was covered with red streaks and purple bruises! I was so amazed when I learned the story I took a picture of him! A week later, the patient was better and he eventually left the hospital (with his colostomy and infected incision). The family, of course, credited the Dong-Y (and Chinese medicine), although I was thankful for the antibiotics!

CHAPTER TWENTY-NINE

MEDCAP TO TUY BÁ

In contacts with the people—follow these three recommendations: To respect the people, To help the people, To defend the people—in order to win their confidence and affection and achieve a perfect understanding between the people and the Army.

People's War, People's Army
—General Vo Nguyen Giap

One day, Major Bowman sent word that he wondered if I'd bring another medical visit to an outlying hamlet. This was further into the U Minh forest and would be "sans nurses." Always eager to get out into the field and see the country firsthand, I quickly said yes. So on Saturday, I arranged for Joe to cover the surgery and went off again.

I reassembled my fatigue gear and sidearms and, early in the morning, Ed Poarch, a lieutenant JG, U.S. Navy type from Louisiana, picked me up and we went to the navy pier, got into the old French gunboat, and headed out into the bay and toward the Gulf of Siam. Then, cutting back up the Song River, we headed inland.

Having been up a good part of the night before, I was tired before we even got started. The land and shore were still beastly hot, and the cool air of the water and the thumping hum of the engines put me to sleep. I curled up behind the cabin and woke up only twice over the next couple of hours. These were the times when we slowed up to gently coast through passes in the fishing nets.

The Vietnamese fishermen had these large nets extending eight to ten feet out of the water, and as deep below, and frequently extending 100 to 150 feet across, blocking the main channels. As the military craft never deliberately got too close to the shore lines, they would have to pass through these nets, and the fisherman would mark the passageways with buoys and tall sticks. The Vietcong, of course, knew this and a favorite trick was to hook a grenade to a wire across the passageway about two or three feet under water. The Vietnamese "people" used sampans, which would easily glide over, and the Vietnamese "military" (ARVN) used bigger, deeper draft vessels, such as the gunboats and junks, and these would trip the wire releasing the firing handle. So going through these areas was always one of a potential problem, and I held onto my life jacket and sat on a metal box—just in case!

At Xeror, we stopped, went ashore, and made a dispensary visit. There were several old people there. I checked for the ARVN sailor who had the mortar frag wounds I'd treated at the compound several weeks before, but no one seemed to know anything about him.

We met *Duiy* (Captain) Cuoi, Major Bowman, Sergeant Nelms, and some ARVN soldiers, transferred into three smaller river assault boats, and went on up the canal.

It was hot as hell, and I was thirsty as all get out, but I was afraid to drink my water so early. I figured the one canteen was going to have to last me all day.

The motor on our boat conked out, and we had to get a tow, further delaying us and causing some anxious moments at the thoughts of being stranded out there!

At Tuy Bá, we stopped. In time for lunch, we went to the ARVN military post, to the subsector chief's quarters. This was a thatched hut, with dirt floor, wooden tables, located inside of the palisaded "fort." Here we had lunch: the inevitable orange soda pop (Segi) with its "typhoid ice" (the man who owned the ice machine must be making a fortune out there!) to drink. The food was rice, shrimp, pork, and cabbage soup, all of which ended up being mixed together in a wooden bowl, held close to the mouth, and shoveled in with chopsticks. I was a real "old China hand" at this by now.

It was hot even under the trees and I couldn't eat much, but the drink tasted good, and, as I had been doing for weeks, I hoped my immunizations were working!

The ARVN's were very hospitable. We needed interpreters, but their conversation was interesting. They laughed a lot and talked loudly to each other or anyone who listened. Major Bowman and Sergeant Helms asked some public health questions regarding sickness in the area or unusual injuries and made notes for reports.

After lunch, we got back into some sampans (the boats and the canals were getting smaller) and proceeded upstream for some thirty minutes.

Suddenly we ducked into the shore, and I became aware we were at the edge of a village and twenty or thirty people were there all around us. The jungle had so effectively hidden them, I hadn't seen them until the last possible moment!

The village leaders and elders came forward and introductions were carried out, although I couldn't have caught any names if my life had depended upon it! They were most polite and gracious. We walked not too far to a building that I was told was the schoolhouse, recently completed. It was basically a bamboo-walled, dirt-floored, thatched-roof, "little grass shack." About fifty people had gathered inside, all sitting on rude benches.

101

(It was to be noted that the village governments composed of tiny hamlets for many years were almost untouched by central government. They were inclined to be opposed to any kind of central authority, whether RVN or VC.)

Diuy Cuoi made a speech, followed by much hand-clapping, and then some of the villagers stood up and spoke, likewise followed by more clapping. Finally they got me up in front and I made a speech, with the *Diuy*, who spoke *excellent* English, French, Vietnamese (and goodness knows what else!) translating. I told them of my "village" at home, brought greetings from my people, then told them I was a doctor, explained I (we) was there to help them with medicines. I told them we wished to show that the Americans and the government of South Vietnam could help them where the Vietcong could not. Again there was much clapping.

Then we set up shop in the front of the building between a large South Vietnamese flag and an American flag. Together with Sergeant Nelms, two ARVN soldiers (whom I gathered must have been some kind of medics), some volunteers from the village, and an interpreter, we spread our medicines on a table, and the patients lined up and came forward one at a time.

There was practically no time to do any real history or examination. Sergeant Nelms and the ARVN seemed to know more about what needed to be done. I could barely ask two or three questions, either listen to the chest, feel the abdomen (standing up), inspect the skin, or feel some part of the body, and then shout out the medicine. One, two, or three minutes per patient, and thus, we processed about a hundred people over the next two hours.

Our medicines were aspirin (aches, pains, fever); diarrhea pills (worms?); vitamins (tired, lethargic, anemic? parasites, malaria, etc.); tranquilizers (headaches and insomnia); worm pills (when described as passing in the stools); sometimes sulfa tablets for obvious infections, boils.

It was hot, noisy, dirty, smelly, constant motion, push and shove. I lost five pounds in weight. Every so often when I stopped to wipe the sweat away, there would be some shouting and gesturing, and I would be supplied with a swig of coconut water (out of the coconut!) to drink. This kept me on my feet until about four o'clock when our team said we had to go.

102

The Vietnamese followed us back to the boats, the children tugging at my uniform, all laughing and chattering and playing around. It was a farewell, just as if I'd been there for weeks, months, or years. I had the notion I was the greatest, dearest friend and they were losing me, and all after only a few, hot, intense hours.

But, this is the way it is in military situations and, I have found over the years, in war. Intense, "until death do us part" type friendships can quickly arise under the moving, shared, stresses of combat. However, I found the Vietnamese people to be the sort that, although they seemed shy, reticent, standoffish, could also be very dependent and make you feel that you had been one among them forever and that they were losing a member of the family and not a stranger.

Our sampans got us back to Tuy Ba (the fort). We held a critique about the day, and the American advisory team was so very pleased and felt it was a successful operation. I was the first *doctor* of any sort to get into the area, and the people were so impressed. I was doubly glad to be able to help out Major Bowman and the advisory team. Also his "radio man" was a pink-cheeked boy who didn't look to be even eighteen, constantly sweating with a radio strapped to his back, running to keep up everywhere. I could picture my own sons in some distant time and hoped maybe someone else would do a kindness to them for me for one day. (If everyone in the world would do one kindness for one period on one day, . . .)

From Tuy Ba, we took the assault boats back to Xeror, and here I left Major Bowman and Diny Cuoi. I have some movies I took from the deck of the gunboat with the two of them standing side by side on the shore, saluting and waving good-bye under the ARVN flag. Two men, of the most totally different backgrounds one could conjure, living a spartan existence, in a jungle insurgency warfare situation with little assistance. I felt so sorry for them, yet so very proud that we could find such soldiers to perform these lonely, lonely, dangerous tasks. I stood and waved back until we were too small to be seen by each other.

I wonder what happened to them?

Nelms rode back with us to Rach Gia. We had to resupply his medical kit before setting out into the bush again. Once more, the ARVN sailors shot up the mangrove swamps, and I tried to doze.

We got back home as the sun was setting, and Sergeant Nelms and I walked over to the BOQ where I left him and hitched a ride back to the hospital and the Bac Si house.

They had all eaten supper and so I had leftovers, but wasn't very hungry as I was too tired and hot. So I tried one of Joe's Vietnamese martinis (there was no vermouth, so we used Japanese Scotch, a half part to four parts of Australian gin). This gave me enough strength to go downtown and get a haircut. Then Jerry and I walked around the town, taking in the local color (nighttime downtown in a Vietnamese province town is some experience) and ended up at the U.S. Military BOQ bar for another drink.

I was finally home and showered and just getting into bed, when a group from the American military advisory team came in, rousted me out and insisted we go to the navy club. This was the local Vietnamese hangout frequented by the U.S. Navy types when they came into port at Rach Gia, after being on swift boat patrols in the Gulf of Siam. We went in and drank *Ba Me Ra* (a Vietnamese French beer that tasted like formaldehyde and left one with a vicious hangover).

Captain Jim Ritchie, a young, eager, paratrooper from Marietta, Ohio, was a challenging conversationalist and regaled us with paratroop stories. Tom ("Shot-gun") Smith of Texas (where else?) and Gary Schnetzler of New York, two of the FAC pilots, threw in flying tales for good contrast.

It was morning before we broke up, and I'd forgotten all about Tuy Ba!

CHAPTER THIRTY

TEKSU

No one,
Only water, clear water.
Look! A sail fluttering,
An oar flapping in the distance.

West Lake, Late Afternoon
—Vietnamese Anonymous (18th century)

We got up at seven, made quick rounds, and all were squared away
and left Joe to cover the house for the day. At eight, we rode
downtown in jeeps to the navy-base area and loaded onto two junks.
There were a number of people from the MAAG team in Rach Gia,
as well as others who were going along for the Sunday holiday.

It was a beautiful, sunny day and once into the gulf, the salt
air smelled invigorating, clean, and fresh. We headed for Turtle
Island (Teksu) about twenty-five miles out in the Gulf of Siam. It
took about one and one-half hours to get through mud flats and to
deep water. We sunbathed, talked, drank beer, and took movies,
very relaxed and pleasant. At Teksu, we patrolled along the shore.
All was quiet and serene, very pretty, looking like a Robinson-
Crusoe setting. We found it was uninhabited.

It was about five miles long, three miles wide, rising 500 feet
out of the water, and resembling a huge, sea-monster turtle. There
wasn't a soul around. About noon, we found a secluded cove and
put in. We had an assault boat on one junk, and it took turns carrying
us all into shore. The nurses had brought beer, sandwiches, and
Coke, and we had a regular picnic. The navy guys had water skis
and, using the assault boat for power, we all took turns.

I had never done it before, but made it up the first time I tried
and had a thrilling ride around the little bay. One of the men
thoughtfully took some movies with my camera. I kept going until
I thought my arms, legs, and back were going to burst! However,
I didn't spill and managed to make a couple of back crosses and ride
the roughest waves. Didn't know what a great sport I'd been missing! I finally had to coast in very tired!

During the afternoon, one of the men fell on the rocks and cut his leg rather badly on the barnacles. We called on a portable radio and contacted one of the Swift boats on patrol. About an hour later, he came into the bay with a first-aid kit, and we were able to fairly definitively take care of the wound. (Later that night back at the hospital, we redebrided it and sewed it up under antibiotic cover.) Later, a second Swift boat, on routine patrol, coming by, saw the conglomeration of boats, and wondering what it meant, came speeding into the bay at battle stations!

They all joined in the fun for a while. Then they offered us a ride.

These Swift boats were sort of the equivalent of World War II PT boats. They had a fifty-foot aluminum hull with twin GM diesel engines and cruised at twenty-one knots with twenty-five knots top speed. They mounted three fifty-caliber machine guns and an 81 mm mortar: very rugged craft. The crews gave us a thrilling ride at high speed (30? mph—on the water; that is fast as hell!). We watched them machine-gun the shoreline—both for practice with their weapons and just to aggravate the "Charlies"—"keep them off balance all the time"—"they never know where US-VN forces will hit"—paying them back at their own game!

One of the captains was a young (twenty-two) lieutenant JG from Charlotte ("home folks") named McCorkle. He seemed so young and lonesome out there, roaming around on an overgrown cabin cruiser, shooting at the VC on shore!

Later on the ocean, we transferred back to our own junks and came home. We landed and stopped first at the BEQ for steak dinner. I was hot, tired, sun and windburned. When I got to the hospital, Joe had a surgical belly waiting for me—a ruptured Meckles diverticulitis. I operated and finally went to bed late.

CHAPTER THIRTY-ONE

VISITORS

Here come Thuong, fellas, shambling along!
Hey, you got any dough, maybe five bucks?
No? maybe three?
I'll pay it back, don't worry, someday I'll pay it back,
Sure.

Borrowing Money
—Dang Tran Thuong (1759–1813)

One of the interesting aspects of the tour was the constant visitation of many different kinds of people and their purposes.

The first day I arrived, there was a U.S. Army medical group that included the USAR-V surgeon-in-chief, inspecting this province hospital deep in the Delta that basically had no connection with the U.S. Army.

A few days later, we had visitors from the International Red Cross in Geneva, Switzerland, again inspecting the hospital with interest in the care given to the Vietcong. (The crowding of eighteen women into ten beds and open toilets for the poor, innocent civilians evidently didn't matter, as long as the murderers were properly cared for!) I could see the hand of the cowardly "do-good-nicks" from the U.S. in this.

There were other volunteer physicians who were interested in how other hospital situations evolved compared to their own: a G.P. from Oregon, a surgeon from the Midwest. One afternoon, in the middle of a big casualty load, Charles Chasler showed up from nowhere! He was the unofficial team leader in San Francisco who didn't have his passport and laid over four days in Hawaii. He had been touring South Vietnam: guess they couldn't find anything else for him to do (radiologists didn't have much to do in the boonies). He served to bring news of all the others, talked incessantly, took lots of pictures, and flew out late in the afternoon.

Joe O'M. said, "My God, doesn't he ever shut up?" Chas was bubbling over with enthusiasm for the total program!

Then there were the military members of other province hospital surgical teams who also wanted to compare notes. The air force colonel who came from Can Tho one day; the Australian surgical team who most of us never saw the day of the great casualty influx.

There were people from the State Department (USAID): One day Dr. Herschell Douglas, the young M.D. medical director from USAID IV Corps flew in for inspection. That day, I had to work him in between a cesarean section, an appendectomy, and a tracheostomy.

We were indeed the Hilton Hotel of the area. Everyone stopped in all the time for coffee, tea, booze, a snack, free meals, etc.

There were also all sorts of military inspection teams. One day a Captain DeLos Santos, a medical service corps officer, from MACV, came through. He traveled around the country, checking on the Regional Force/Popular Force medical channels and supply lines. He had interesting stories to tell, as he had been in the Special Forces before being assigned to his present job.

One of the nicest and best visitors we ever had was the official U.S. Navy-Marine artist, Charles Waterhouse. He was a free-lance artist from Edison, New Jersey. He did sketches of the hospital and the people. It was fascinating to watch him sketch off a picture in the time it takes to set and pose a camera shot.

However, of all the visitors we had, the most infamous was the photographer who touched off the famous napalm burn story. It came about this way.

CHAPTER THIRTY-TWO

"NAPALM, NAPALM . . ."

Life is dirt, in war,
A bullet flies by,
An arrow drops by accident.
Your souls are like fireflies now,
Crying ache in the darkness, for justice.

Calling the Lost Souls
—Nguyen Du (1765–1826)

It was a Sunday morning and there was no elective operating, and we'd been up so as to go to the Roman Catholic services and then make rounds on the patients. One of the aides came running over to the ward, calling "Bac Si, come, Bac Si, come." I looked at him with questioning, and he replied, "She have many burn, many burn. Phom Khu Khop."

I left our little group and hurried across the compound to the E.R. to find it in the usual state of utter confusion that always accompanied the sudden arrival of more than two patients!

(Two patients seemed to be the limit for the crew to handle; add just one more, big or small, and their families of course, and the place just fell apart!)

The three people assigned (a nurse and two aides) could cope with two injuries—even big problems, but let them have one more patient and they called out the entire group of potential help, and then everyone was in everyone else's way!

Anyhow, this was the scene I was expecting, and I wasn't wrong—it was chaos, and perhaps with some good reason.

There lay nine patients with gasoline thermal burns.

One lady had 95 percent total body and died before the day was out. Two others died in the next two days. The others were still in the hospital, suppurating and sick, when I left Vietnam some weeks later.

It seems as if a gasoline tank at a gas station down near the Bus Plaza had exploded—probably a cigarette or static spark—never any hint of sabotage or foul play.

There was a big crowd of people around this section of the plaza, and these poor unfortunates had been the ones to catch the full blast.

I was trying to get I.V.'s started on the ones who looked as if they had a chance for survival, keep the nurses from wasting their time on the obviously terminal, except for giving them morphine and trying to keep the families from smearing them with oily mixtures.

Into the middle of this mass confusion crowded a long-haired, bearded, dirty-clothed American with his camera gear screaming, "Napalm, napalm!" I had noticed him around the hospital the past day and knew he had bummed some meals and a bed out of us, but really hadn't paid very much attention. (There were always so many coming and going. . . .)

Now he came into full focus, setting up his tripod, setting up lights, adjusting his camera, cursing the Vietnamese who were getting in the way, nurses and families, all the while yelling, "They've been napalmed, they've been napalmed!" (i.e., American military forces had done something wrong to the civilians).

We finally brought some order to all this and demonstrated that this had nothing really to do with the war; nothing to do with the Vietcong, the ARVN, or American military; it was strictly a tragic accident, in a town in Vietnam.

I have never seen greater disappointment.

"You mean they weren't napalmed?"

"No."

He hastily folded all his gear, packed it up, and left without taking a single picture!

I wondered how many towns in the United States on any one day in March had a filling-station, gasoline-tank explosion that seriously injured nine people? Such a story would have been major local news, probably prominent statewide news, and perhaps even of nationwide mention.

An even greater news worthiness I thought was the fact that here in a foreign country, in a God-forsaken part of the earth, white, Christian, Westerners were taking care of the medical needs of yellow, Buddhist Orientals, basically charitably, in the middle of a war, and this jerk couldn't see that!

110

All he really wanted was: to do or say or show something that he felt would be to the discredit not just of the military, but to America!

I believe that I felt or saw this happen more than once and especially in later times when I was there again.

It seemed as if the people telling the story to the people back home never tried to find any good to tell. They deliberately looked for the worst things that would make their own country look bad and reported those!

As the years went by, I came to feel that the news media had so wrongfully reported and slanted the news of the entire Vietnamese war that after the fall of South Vietnam (when the North would have a free hand eradicating anything pre-Southern), very little of the true picture of the war would ever come out.

CHAPTER THIRTY-THREE

PALM SUNDAY SERGEANT

Spring dies, the hundred flowers scatter.
Spring is reborn, the hundred flowers bloom.
It is hard for me to see clearly,
Old age blinks my eyes.
Aren't flowers dead, once spring dies?
Last night, out there in the yard, a plum
Branch blossomed.

Rebirth
—Man Giac

Having worked hard during the morning and having been called out several times during the night, I was tired by lunchtime. The help was gone and I cooked myself an omelet, then lay down on the sea wall outside the house to sun, read, and daydream.

About 3:30, the TOC (Tactical Operating Center over at the Military Assistance Advisory Group Headquarters) called us by telephone, saying that a helicopter was bringing in a badly wounded

American soldier and would land at the Short Strip in five minutes. We grabbed a bottle of Dextram and Ringer's, hopped into the jeep, and had a hairy five-minute ride to the strip with me driving. The chopper had already landed, and they were off-loading the patient.

I checked him quickly and knew at a glance he was in bad shape; he was cold, clammy, ashen—badly shocked with an opened, sucking chest wound—he was dying. One of the accompanying soldiers was giving him air-bag breathing. We took long enough to plug the chest leak and start the Dextran, loaded him onto the jeep, and had another wild ride back to the hospital and into the surgery. Here we got some more I.V.'s going, along with oxygen and a blood pressure and improvement in color.

I knew he'd never make it to Saigon (the nearest U.S. Army hospital) by any method of transportation, and we'd have to do the best we could. Luckily, we had a couple of pints of O-negative blood on hand, so within ten minutes, we were pumping the blood and had chest tubes in. Within twenty-five minutes, we had him ready to operate. The MAAG team members scouted around town to find us some O-negative troopers. He had the worst injuries I yet had seen. The high velocity bullets (AK-47 in this instance) do tremendous damage. He had one entrance through the left chest and one through the left flank. There were triple lacerations of the lung, a blow out of the left colon, spleen, and pancreas with tremendous fecal contamination. There were also through and through rents in the stomach and diaphragm. How he lived I don't know, except that he was tough and in good shape. In three and one-half hours, I did a partial pneumonectomy, splenectomy, partial colectomy with separate colostomies, distal pancreatectomy, suture of stomach and diaphragm, and multiple drains and twelve units of blood—all we could muster. I got him off the table, and he survived the night.

It turned out that he was Master Sergeant Glenn Lane of the Special Forces.

He was a fifteen-to sixteen-year professional soldier who had been the 82nd Air Borne "Trooper of the Year" some years before. He had served in the Korean War, had been wounded, had served one tour before in Vietnam, and been wounded again. This event was in the early part of his second tour. He had recruited and trained his guerrilla force in Saigon, and they had been conducting hit-and-run raids on the VC in the Three Sisters area.

He was a team leader of an A-team, composed of mercenaries recruited in Cholon (Hoa-Hao, Kit Carsons, KKK, Cambodian Bandits, and ex VC). They were fighting their guerrilla warfare over in the Three Sisters mountain area about twenty-five miles away when he was wounded.

Years later, when I found out all the details to this story, it seems that one of Sergeant Lane's men had been wounded (a Vietnamese), and an American "Dust-off" chopper had responded and was about to land. Lane and some of his men were clearing brush to give the chopper landing space. Lane said he straightened up from his work and looked up the hill, just as a VC raised up from behind a pile of rocks and let go with an automatic burst. He saw his assailant and knew he had been mortally wounded! The remainder of the team opened on the sniper who skeedaddled, and the chopper immediately sat down. They threw Lane and the other wounded man on, and two of the team clambered aboard and they took off. Once airborne, it became apparent to the men that Lane was dying, and so they radioed to their control net "what to do?" (At this time, 1967, there were no major U.S. combat units in the Delta and really very few U.S. military of any type, and the closest medical support was Saigon—over 100 miles away.) It just so happened that the radio in our TOC was being monitored that Sunday afternoon by a man who was familiar with the medical situation at the province hospital here at Rach Gia. He was caught in the excitement about a chopper going into a fire fight on the Three Sisters, so he broke in the transmission and told them there was a civilian American surgeon at the Vietnamese province hospital at Rach Gia, which they were just about overhead. The pilot figured there was nothing to lose, and hence, the rest of the events.

The American civilian and military personnel around Rach Gia responded wonderfully to our call for blood. I was beat out at midnight. We had spent practically all of the past three days in the operating room, and there seemed to be no end in sight. The Green Beret sergeant incidentally lived in Fayetteville, North Carolina, and I hope maybe to stop by there sometime.

113

MONDAY

"Lots of admissions. My Sergeant doing fine today and arrangements made to air evac him out to the Third Field Hospital tomorrow . . . "

TUESDAY

"At 1300 the Air Evac chopper came. We took Sgt. Lane to the Short Strip and saw him off to the Army hospital in Saigon. He was doing well. Certainly a brave, stout fellow. He'd asked us not to take his boots off when he woke up in the recovery room because he wanted to die with his boots on! Now he apologized for that and said he was sorry to leave us and wished he could have stayed with us in Rach Gia! . . . "

CHAPTER THIRTY-FOUR

THE PROVINCE CHIEF

Pigeon, little pigeon, let me tell you:
Where are you from? Why come here?
You expect a nice cage, a beautiful China bowl,
But you might end up on a chopping board.

Pigeon
—Nguyen Quy Tan

One afternoon, Joe and I were called to go over to the province chief's house. Actually, Joe had seen him medically a couple of times before, but, because of being a very limited surgical specialist in plastic surgery, Joe felt a little uneasy and asked me to go along. I think he wanted not only some other medical opinion, but also reinforcements for whatever he might have to say!

I had passed by the province chief's villa numerous times. It was on the other side of town and, on the way to the MAAG BOQ or TOC, we would drive or walk by. I had wondered what it would be like inside the large gates. The house was set well back off the street and had large grounds surrounding it, all enclosed by a high, spiked, iron-rail fence. In the corners of the compound were guard boxes, and there were rolls of barbed wire (concertian) strung all around. There were guards at the gate, examining all who came in or left. (The little "mirror men.") Within the compound, along the drive in front of the house was always parked a jeep or two with mounted machine guns or an APC with the inevitable soldier with the inevitable cigarette dangling from his lips, sort of half reclining behind the .50 caliber. Around the grounds were generally various kinds of military people.

At night, it was one of the most lighted places in Rach Gia.

Joe drove the jeep. We were both in civilian clothes when we came up to the gate. The guards, of course, didn't comprehend a word we were saying or even pretend to try to understand our signs and "pig-Latin" Vietnamese.

However, they recognized us as the American doctors from the hospital and let us through, rather lackadaisically, I thought.

We drove up to the front steps, which led up to a wide veranda, got out and walked up. There was no one at the front door, so we went inside and into a large anteroom type of hallway. It had high ceilings—two story with numerous rooms coming off it and at the back a gorgeous double staircase—like something from a movie set and one momentarily expected to see some Southern beauty descend the steps in her hooped skirt. I was impressed, and Joe said he thought I'd be!

We were standing by a large table underneath a large chandelier, enjoying the coolness of the place, for it must have been twenty-five to thirty degrees cooler inside than out, when a smiling, young *Diuy* (Captain) bounded out of one room and welcomed us in flawless English!

He and Joe seemed to know each other—possibly from other visits, but Joe being so bad for names didn't bother to introduce me. We exchanged a few pleasantries about the weather, the hospital, Colonel Bellinger and my recent Med Cap. Then the captain told us Major Dom was waiting. We followed into another room.

This was a large parlor-sitting room that was being used as an office. Large windows, ground-to-ceiling-French-style, opened on the other side to an outside garden. There were at least two armed guards out there who didn't pay us too much attention.

We were introduced to Major Dom, who was standing and gave us a short smiling bow of his head. The Major was young—thirty-four—we later found out. He was also the brother-in-law of the IV Corps commander. Nepotism was rampant in South Vietnam, as it seems to be throughout the Orient.

We came to understand that the province chief was not only like a civil governor of a geographic area (appointed and not elected!), but also the military commander of all the Vietnamese military forces in the area. As such, he was a dictator—lord and master of Kein Giang Province. Colonel Bellinger was his American counterpart and had to work with him, put up with his whims and idiosyncrasies, and somehow give him advice on how the Americans thought the war ought to be won.

Some of the chiefs were reluctant to fight and did not like to commit their men to operations. Their few resources, they frequently like to hoard to protect themselves and their friends. Trying to get some of them to fight was difficult at times. Of course, they couldn't afford to have too many losses among the "Rough-Puffs," i.e., the home militia forces, or the chief would certainly lose whatever popularity he might have locally.

Major Dom was only a major because he had not yet amassed enough money to buy himself a higher commission! This notion of what we would call "graft" was the bane of Americans trying to evaluate, work with, and justify their positions with the South Vietnamese. However, "Cumshaw" is an Oriental custom to which they attach no moral value, it is neither a "good" nor a "bad." It is just the way things get done! The Americans who got all ethically upset by the under-the-table payments of money or favors ended up by being ineffective in their dealings with the Vietnamese. We had to learn to accept them as they were—after all, we wouldn't change them in one year or ten. As I was frequently reminded, we were the barbarians (with a history of two hundred years), and they the civilized ones (with a history of two thousand years!).

As Major Dom spoke no English, the *Diuy* translated for us, and it was one of those amusing experiences I have previously written about. It turned out our patient had the "bellyache." I asked some questions relating to various parts of his anatomy and felt I could localize the problem as being of gallbladder, stomach, duodenal, pancreative, nature. We did a limited abdominal examination, with the patient lying on a couch; we checked his heart, lungs, throat, and blood pressure.

Talking to each other as we went along, Joe and I decided the fellow had either a "nervous stomach" or a peptic ulcer. Of course, we needed some simple laboratory tests of the blood and stool examination, but these really wouldn't have been of too much added value, as most Vietnamese had intestinal parasites (bellyache and blood in stools and possible/anemia!). A GI-series barium X-ray examination was out of the question. I doubt it could have been done even in Saigon in those days.

After seeing his life-style, finding out his background, and discovering that the previous two province chiefs had been killed by the VC, Joe and I decided Major Dom had ample reason to have a duodenal ulcer gnawing at his vitals. The situation around him certainly was!

CHAPTER THIRTY-FIVE

THE THREE SISTERS

The gods do not subtract from man's allotted time the hours spent in flying.

About one o'clock, I drove out to the short strip with Ted ("Sky King") and Gary S. the two FAC (Forward Air Controller) pilots. I flew in the rear seat of the plane with Sky. These were the L-19's, which are a big version of the Piper Cub-like planes. They are stressed for G-forces and more powerfully engined. The Vietnamese mechanics turned the props over; Sky helped me into the seat harness (no parachutes) ("If anything happens with what we'll be doing, a parachute won't get you anywhere."), told me to keep hands and feet off the controls, and showed me how to use the radio headset so we could talk with each other. Then he and Gary each taxied out into the grass strip and took off together in formation, as they frequently did.

We made a steep, circling, quick climb over Rach Gia and then headed northwest to the vicinity of the Three Sisters Mountains. This was where Sergeant Lane had been ambushed the week before.

Within fifteen minutes, the mountains were in sight; good-sized hills rising sharply from the flat delta. Approaching them, Sky found two sampans going down a canal; and shouting, "VC," he did a tight turn and a descending spiral. At about 800 feet, Sky reached under the seat and pulled out a grenade, pulled the pin, put the plane in a sharp bank, and dropped it! He then pulled up into a sharp climb that pushed me into the seat, and I felt as if I couldn't move. He then told me to reach under my seat and pull out a box containing signal grenades. Showing me how to pull the pin, he yelled for me to hold on, put the aircraft into a steep turn, and leaning over the side, he let it go! (The sides were down—this is the way they flew.) He made a diving turn down to about 500 feet, again tilted the plane on its side (I felt like I was falling out), and repeated the sequence. Another tight bank, followed by a gradually shallow turn, and we watched the smoke trail until it hit the shore about twenty-five feet from the sampans and burst into flames. We climbed for altitude until he got another grenade ready, and we repeated the maneuver. This time he was even wider of the mark. Seeing that he was no bombardier today, Sky climbed out of the area!

As we flew along, he told me that what we were doing was called the RAND Bombing Technique: Right About Now Drop!

We then flew on toward the Three Sisters. Spotting a thin rising curl of wood smoke on the lower slope of the nearest hill, Sky yelled, "Tally ho," and put the plane in a sharp dive at high speed. As we got close in, he pointed out that this indicated a cooking fire, hence a camp, and only the VC were in these hills, so everything was fair game. As we closed in, he fired one rocket with a mighty swoosh that caused us to weave from the recoil. Then he turned into a climbing turn, and we leaned out the other side to watch the hit. However, because of the steepness of the turn and the contour of the hill, we couldn't see; but our number-two plane, coming in behind, radioed that we'd missed the target! He also said he was taking small-arms fire.

Sky peeled the L-19 around and made a steeper approach—I thought he was going to run into the side of the hill. He demonstrated the rocket-firing device while he flew and aimed the aircraft; then he yelled and fired the rockets. (We had four all together.) On the second and third runs, we heard this "pinging" sound, and Sky said we had been hit! (Sure enough, when we landed later, we had three bullet holes in our wings and elevators—it looked like a small-caliber carbine weapon.) After he had shot off all the rockets, Sky flew cover for Gary to make his runs. The eight rockets hit generally in the vicinity of the campfire smoke, but it was still burning when we left, and Gary's plane was hit. (Several days later, he took a round through the floor of his plane, and it furrowed the calf of his leg, putting him out of commission for a while!)

As we were now beginning to get toward the end of the allotted flying time, we headed home, and Sky did some map-of-the-earth flying down the canals and across the rice paddies, looking to see if he could spot any changes or activities.

I was bushed from the tension and excitement and that night I slept poorly, feeling as if I were G-forcing all night, pushing through the floor of the plane.

CHAPTER THIRTY-SIX

SURGICAL PRACTICE

You sat and planned out battles,
Schemed for command,
Blew up thunder and lightning,
Killed millions to make your glory.
Battles turned wrong, a stray arrow, a chance bullet,
And your blood on the field, your flesh rots.

Calling the Lost Souls
—Nguyen Du

The majority of our work was related to trauma, and almost all of that was secondary to war injuries. Of all the cases I operated on, almost all were caused by gunshot or missile fragments. I did all the abdominal cases and many of the amputations. The open fractures and debridements were handled by the orthopedic surgeon. Our policy was to operate on all of these casualties. Because there were so few of us to operate, and having such scanty and inadequate help and very little laboratory help, we felt that "watchful waiting" was not in the best interest of these patients. All our head wounds, with or without skull fractures, were treated nonoperatively. The solitary chest injuries were, for the most part, managed by closed thoracotomy chest tubes to underwater bottles. (No suction available.) All the thoraco-abdominal wounds were open explored and in the course of any two-month period, every abdominal organ or a portion thereof had been removed at least once!

The open-fracture treatment was to debride the wounds, pack them open, and use some sort of external immobilization, either splints and/or plaster casting. A fair number of amputations were done, as we had scanty antibiotic resources (save the penicillin) and did not have the facilities or help in attempting to salvage a limb.

The worst injuries were the paraplegics. There was little hope for them, because of the long-term problem and need for good nursing management and care. The matter of getting them out of bed, urinary bladder care, bowel care, and skin care was just a horrendous job that simply there weren't enough people to carry out. (Oh, there were plenty of bodies, but finding dedicated people to keep at these jobs was difficult. The families would soon tire of all the extra burden and allow nature to not-so-mercifully take its course.)

Some of the peculiar injuries we saw were the punji-stick wounds and water-buffalo-horn wounds.

The punji stick was a small, fire-hardened, sharpened piece of wood, that had been dipped in human or animal feces and set in the ground in shallow pits. It was angled so that it would pierce the foot or ankle area and caused an agonizing injury and chronic infetion. It led to a low-grade, smoldering cellulitus or osteomyelitis that lingered painfully for months and responded poorly to antibiotics. On any ward, one could also see half a dozen patients with a foot propped up, covered with bandages soaked in Dakin's solution.

The water-buffalo-horn injuries were like those of the bullfighters: hooking, slashing stab wounds about the groin, genitalia, or rectal areas.

The most common nontraumatic surgical condition of the abdomen was appendicitis. It seemed to me to be rather common. In all the cases we saw, the appendix was ruptured and the patient had peritonitis when operated upon. Nearly all of these people said they had been sick "a few days." Occasionally, we would operate on a patient with advanced peritonitis who said he had been sick only one day! I felt that it was probably that to the average Vietnamese, whose intestinal tract harbored various parasites anyhow, physical discomfort of his abdomen was so "normal" that the pain of obstructive appendicitis was of little consequence. He really got a worse pain when his inflamed appendix finally burst and peritonitis ensued—then it was time to see the doctor! (This fitted well with our overall feeling that the Vietnamese never sought medical help until things were in an advanced stage of the disease. By contrast in America, the patients run to the doctor so early in the course of a disease process, he can't diagnose it by standard or usual methods!) Because of the low-carbohydrate diet, most of the patients did not have much anorexia or vomiting.

At operation, 90 percent of those ruptured appendices were anatomically retrocecal, which just made for a difficult operative procedure.

We saw a large number of women with huge ovarian tumors. As we had no way of identifying the tissue pathologically, we were never really certain whether we were dealing with cancer or not.

Another interesting abdominal surgical condition I encountered was the ruptured ulcer of a typhoid enteritis. (Typhoid fever is barely mentioned in modern American, medical-school training, yet it was relatively common in South Vietnam, and, therefore, its complications.) Although cultures of the blood are diagnostic during the first week of illness with typhoid fever, a stool culture diagnostic in the second week, and the Widal blood test positive by the third week, none of these modalities were available to us. Therefore, we relied on the Vietnamese doctors to make the diagnosis clinically.

Abscesses and infections of the soft tissues were very common, and we did a lot of draining and packing.

We saw a lot of large, apparently colloid, goiters. The prevalence of this condition in this seacoast town with lots of fish available to eat (iodine) was peculiar. Most of these people wouldn't let you operate upon them.

Another interesting conditio. we ran into was large bladder stones. It was felt that long-standing borderline dehydration in the tropical environment plus something about the water (either more or less of some chemical) cause a precipitate in a urine of high specific gravity.

Some of the things we *did not* encounter, or see, I felt were perhaps as interesting, or as telling, about the health of these people. For example, we did not do any gallbladder surgery, very little peptic ulcer surgery, no varicose vein surgery, and no breast surgery.

As mentioned earlier, we had no way to pathologically (histologically) diagnose cancer. One team member figured up, over a seven-month period of more than 900 operations and 2,500 patients, only twelve cases of cancer were seen.

Also, more striking, during the three years the surgical team had been at Rach Gia, *no* tonsillectomy or adenoidectomy had been performed. (There is probably no 600-bed, acute-care hospital in the United States that could make such a statement, ever!)

Some of the nonsurgical conditions we encountered and were exposed to were tuberculosis, malaria, parasites, and congenital deformities.

The Ministry of Health estimated in the mid-1960s that one third of the population of South Vietnam had infectious tuberculosis! Outside of the constant danger of being exposed to it (I suppose all of us had positive tuberculin tests before we ever got to Vietnam!), we occasionally encountered tuberculous peritonitis in a patient being operated upon for abdominal pain. These patients healed their incision O.K., but we had no drug therapy and the patients were lost to any sort of follow-up.

Malaria was not common in the Rach Gia area. Of course, all the Americans took malaria prophylaxis (with its constant GI upset effects) and occasionally at surgery, I would note a large, hard, malarious spleen.

What was very common was parasitic infestation. Almost all the Vietnamese patients had worms. We felt this partly explained the high incidence of anemia in the population. At surgery of gunshot wounds of the intestines, frequently there were all sorts of worms crawling out the holes! Ascaris, trichuria, and hookworm especially!

Amebiasis rarely presented us with a distinct surgical problem. A chronic low-grade diarrhea was so common as to be almost normal. We had proctoscopes that occasionally worked, but rarely was intestinal amebiasis definitively diagnosed. We did see extra colonic amebomas (tumors caused by the amebic parasite infection) of the skin.

Congenital deformities seemed rather common, and particularly so was the cleft lip; also imperforate anus. The reconstructive surgery of grafting for burns, revising scars, contractures, and closing wounds could have kept a plastic surgeon busy forever, it seemed! As a matter of fact, our medical-team leader was a plastic surgeon, and this drew a lot of patients into this hospital for these elective procedures. In particular, the *cleft-lip operation* was our medical psychological warfare procedure.

The Vietnamese view deformities as signs of the disfavor of God and tend to have little to do with the victim. With a large number of the cleft-lip children available and the operation relatively simple in the hands of a well-trained plastic surgeon, we felt we had a good thing going. The older children would cooperate for a local anesthesia supplemented by oral sedation, and the smaller kiddies we could give a general endotracheal anesthesia. We felt that this operation, which so enhanced the good looks of a child who looked rather hideous, demonstrated to the local population that the Americans and the South Vietnamese governments could do for them what the Viet Cong and the North Vietnamese could not do. This fitted right into the American Armed Forces Psychological Warfare Program. Jerry H. and I spent a number of hours making an eight mm movie of the procedure.

All in all, I felt that it was as if I'd gotten into a medical time machine and traveled back in time a hundred years medically! My long-dead grandfather, a country doctor in rural Piedmont, Carolina, would have been more at ease (and perhaps a better "doctor") with these people and their diseases than I was, except for the war trauma!

I was sorry that, scientifically, American medicine had done so little to investigate it all. For example, many of the diseases, long nonexistent in American medicine, were rampant here and just aching for good scientific investigation!

CHAPTER THIRTY-SEVEN

AT THE LAST

It isn't lightning, or the beating of rain,
I'm simply sad, night after night.
Ah, I might as well sleep, the devil with
Insomniacs, night-prowlers, priests, students.
Hear: my bald-headed friend is whacking the temple bells.

Night Sadness
—Tran Te Xeong (1869–1907)

I surely did hate the thought of leaving the team and the work. It had been so stimulating and exciting. I was fearful for the team, in that Joe was getting worse every day with his drinking. The night before, he fell down a couple of times, stumbling around the kitchen. He had gotten to where he would get so bloody smashy and sentimental and start shooting his mouth off about the "Congo," etc. He could get some of the wildest, hare-brained, ideas and would pay only half attention what was said to him. He stayed in a fog many a day. At least, we could count on him forgetting most of the ridiculous things he said with the passage of a few hours. He would carry on sort of half-conversations, with things only partly explained, and interpreted with some obtuse or unrelated thought or story and then promptly forget what he had started today. Bob R., Jerry H., and the nurses wanted me to see Captain Burke (USN) or Colonel Moncrief when I went to Saigon and put in a word of caution.

The last night, I was afraid they would almost come to blows! There was a swell going-away party for me. Betty Crocker cooked a Vietnamese dinner with *nuoc mam* and all. The team broke out a bottle of champagne, and we toasted all around. The "In-group," Joe, Bob, Jerry, Dennis, Bev, Kathy, Winnie, Anne, Sky, and Gary all gathered around. Sister Clotilde of the nuns came around to wish me *bon voyage*. Lieutenant Skilket of the navy and "Flash" Gordon for the army groups came by the house to say good-bye for their groups. Everyone got slightly tanked. We sang songs, told jokes,

125

and talked about leaving. I did one tape recording and took some pictures.

Joe went into his room right after supper. About 11:15 Anne, Jerry H., and I were sitting and listening to her play the guitar and singing, and the rest were in the front of the house or out on the seawall when Joe burst out saying, "I want to see Commander immediately."

He went off into a long harangue on "seabags and bedrolls," "rocks and shoals," it was going to be "strictly GI from here on out." There would be no sleeping late (referring to Bob R.'s occasionally oversleeping at times!) and that when he (Joe) said, "Fall out," he meant "Fall out," even at 5 A.M.! He was wild and fogged out of it!

Jerry was just tight enough and fed up enough to come back at him and said he wasn't getting up on his day off for anyone, and he'd sleep as late as he wanted to if there was no surgery. They almost came to blows, and I had to get in between them to get them apart.

Joe told Jerry if he didn't like things he could get out—get transferred. They were really going at it, and then Joe lit into Anne. She is a fierce war-horse when attacked, and it took me fifteen minutes to break it up and get them out of the house and back into his room. Then we all went over to the Co Bac Si (nurses) house and tried to get everyone quieted down.

Bob R. went back to the house, talked to Joe, and told him we all knew he was an alcoholic and that he was tearing the team apart and he'd have to change.

We were up at 3 A.M. thrashing the problem out, and I promised to see the big boys in Saigon and do what I could, at least say something. Needless to say, it was a sort of distasteful thing to happen on the last night.

Anyhow, the gang gave me a captured VC flag with their names on it, and the military promised me a memento. The navy "awarded" me a plaque, and the hospital civilians gave me a genuine Vietnamese rice knife.

CHAPTER THIRTY-EIGHT

HET ROI

O majestic lands
Where our holy race ruled,
Where I knew freedom,
Where I will never come again!
Lying in this weariness
I still dream great forest dreams,
And my soul comes to you—
O lovely jungles, o mine!

Green Nostalgia
—Nguyen thi Lu

I slept very little and felt crummy after getting up at an early hour. However, I had a few patients for whom I wanted to go over plans for their continued care and good-byes to a few of the Vietnamese people.

I did my last-minute chores, cleaned out my desk, and packed. I left some items with Dennis and Jerry and some of my clothing with Bendix and Westinghouse. Dr. Tuan came by to say good-bye.

I had a short operative schedule and had things planned so as to be picked up after lunch. The one item that USAID Headquarters had been most firm and insistent about was that when our time was up and they sent for us to come out, there was to be no diddling around with the schedule. We were to get out!

We had a fast lunch of the inevitable chicken-noodle soup, spam, and bananas. I'll never eat those without thinking of Vietnam!

At 1:30, we went to the Short Strip.

Many of the hospital personnel came by, and there was much "good-bying," many pictures taken, and recollections of events and happenings.

I could not stall it any longer, as I was the only passenger and the helio pilot was anxious to move along. I climbed aboard and sat with the pilot. He had very little warm-up and a short takeoff roll. As was customary, to give the VC very little target of opportunity, the pilot put the plane into sharp, steep, climbing turn over town.

I was very sad.

Good-bye, hospital: dirty, smelly, hot, with your festering arms and legs; your wormy guts, rats, flies, and mosquitos. Good-bye Bac Si house and afternoon Rob Roys; good-bye, Westinghouse, Betty Crocker, Bendix, spam, pineapple and bananas, buffalo meat and rice. Good Tome, Seagull and your unhousebroken habits, so long and good luck! (The Vietnamese eat dogs, you know); good-bye to the marketplace, barbershop, bridges, smelly canals and hot, hot streets; good-bye and good luck, army, navy, air force, you bright young men tired of flirting with death and longing for home; good-bye, water, rice, dirt and heat. Good-bye to diarrhea, dysentery, dermatitis; good-bye to fish, filth, feces, and flies; good-bye, booze, and brawls; good-bye, disease, death, and disaster.

I loved you all.

Two circles around, we were up to 4,000 feet, and Rach Gia disappeared into the haze.

CHAPTER THIRTY-NINE

SAIGON AGAIN

They say: Pho Hien, more fun than the capital.
After three days I say: there's nothing, nothing,
Just little chinks, old chinks, chinks with white teeth,
And whores with black-bottomed skirts!

Pho Hien
—Trang Quynh

In forty minutes of easy flight, we were in Can Tho. There I switched to a Twin Beech, again the only passenger. We had a plane load of supplies for Long Xuygen and were supposed to pick up someone there. However, after we landed, no one showed up. It must have been 120 degrees in the shade, and the pilot went into a little shelter building, lay down on a bench, and went to sleep! There was not a soul around, no other aircraft, nothing, lonely as all get out! About one half mile away was an ARVN outpost of some sort. I wandered around, getting a little fidgety, took some pictures, and, figuring the pilot must know something, I lay down on one of the benches and exhausted from the tension, excitement, and lack of sleep, I too dozed off.

I was startled awake by the pilot who said it was time to go. No one had ever shown up! We boarded the plane and, in forty minutes, we were landing at busy Ton Son Nhut.

I grabbed my two suitcases, found a USAID bus, and after several stops, made my way back to 191 Cong Ly.

The Can Tho group and several others were already in, and everyone was bubbling over with excitement about their tours. All wanted to talk at once and tell of their experiences. We had a couple of beers and others arrived. About seven o'clock, we all walked together to the Hotel Duc where we had a fine air-conditioned meal. I had a martini and steak, and were they good!

Our conclusions for the evening were that we should win the war, get the country on its feet, and get the hell out!

Saigon was still the same noisy, hot, dirty, bustling, and crowded place. We stayed up late, talking and laying plans about getting home.

I could barely get to sleep. The room was small and hot, the bed hard, and the noise outside seemed overwhelming. I just couldn't relax and get settled down, still too keyed up.

The next morning, we went to Dr. Phelps' office at the Mondial Hotel where we were officially "debriefed," turned in our reports, and were presented with certificates.

I proposed two things: (1) they should screen out doctors whose approach seems to be too rigid, and (2) they should emphasize that we, who represented Western medicine, must often gracefully accept a secondary role to the Chinese-medicine doctor.

Dr. Phelps then gently chided me for flying U.S. Air Force combat missions! Then the assistant, John Miller, took us to get our passports and airlines tickets. We went to the Rex BOQ for lunch.

I went out, walked the streets, took pictures, and shopped. It was very hot, and I was sweating to beat the band. We could still hear bombing to the north, jets overhead, and the constant traffic noise, all sort of overpowering after the quietness out in the province. But that was now all behind.

Everyone was very enthusiastic about the program, what they saw and did, but now all were ready to get the hell out! I spent the afternoon talking with the fellows and writing. Several of the doctors left: Ed Green to Cairo; Tatem to Hong Kong; Behringer to Paris; Sam Walker to Australia; and Lewis back to Hawaii.

We spent our last night again at the Hotel Duc for another delicious air-conditioned meal and marveled at the many Western-European types present. It was a slow walk back along the still-crowded streets. The street traffic noise was almost intolerable until midnight, and I couldn't get to sleep. Thank goodness it was the last night, and I was glad to get out of here. (A few years later, I would learn the G.I.'s had a phrase for all this, "short-timers syndrome.")

The traffic, resuming with passing convoys, scooters, trucks honking their horns, and gunning motors, groggily brought me awake. Up, breakfasted, packed, and out to Ton Sun Nhut.

Miller, Welsh, Kimbrough, and myself blew our last piasters on *Ba Muoi Ba* (Beer), passed through customs, and climbed aboard an Air Vietnam Caravelle. We were on the ground a long time in a long line of traffic and as I looked out at the Pan Am jets arriving, the helicopters and military jets waiting to take off along with the Helios and Dorniers, I wondered if out there somewhere was my replacement.

I never met him!

CHAPTER FORTY

AROUND THE WORLD AND HOME

Old—and so much still to do.
Heaven and earth is too vast: drink up!
With luck even fool wins glory,
Without it a hero is helpless.
I fought like my lord, dreamt of holding the earth's axis:
There's no way to reach the heavenly river.

Regrets
—Dang Dung

The trip home "on around the world" was yet another fantastic adventure and was something from the dream pages of any travel agent.

From Saigon, we went via Air Vietnam in a Caravelle jet to Phnom Penh, Cambodia, where our stay was no more than an airport visit, then on to Bangkok. There was one of the easiest customs I encountered. We got a room at the military hotel, walked around town, had dinner at a Thai restaurant, and did much sight-seeing. My final diary comment for the day was, "to bed very tired and glad to be out of Vietnam in one piece."

The next several days were given over to intensive sight-seeing and gift-buying under the surveillance of a man named "Johnny." He picked the four of us out at the hotel, furnished the car, excellent English, a knowledge of what four American bachelors on the town wanted to see and do, and a spirit of fun for his own country and town. We toured the *Klongs* (canals), floating markets, Wat Arun, many other temples and buildings, silk making, elephants at forestry work, sword fighting (fantastic), Thai boxing, the Pasteur Institute and snake farm, cock fighting, their dancing, government buildings, to Bang-Pi-In (the old summer capital), Ayudyha (the olden times capital), the Emerald Buddha and many other places. It was hot, but the streets were clean, well lit at night, and the buildings and signs were fresh (they had had the Summer Olympics there a few years before and were still spruced up for the G.I.'s coming on R & R from 'Nam).

At Bang-Pi-In, I had the most interesting and intense *déjà vu"* experience I guess I've had. We were walking across an open lawn between several of the buildings and a little lake. In the distance not too far was a bandstand, covered over sitting in the trees. An orchestra of young Thais were playing the Malaysian musical instrument called the *Ang-Kalung*. This instrument has three bamboo pipes of various sizes and lengths with a rattle and, when shaken, produces a hollow-to-tinkling sound of the scale. Each player has one in each hand and it would take ten to twelve players to be able to produce music. The music is the most beautiful, haunting, sound I've ever heard and produced a tremendous nostalgia, very intense and sudden. I *knew*—(knew in the sense that I know the sun will rise and set, two plus two equals four, etc.) I knew that I had been in *that* place before!! It took me several days to get over the experience.

Before leaving, we visited SEATO Headquarters and the Medical Laboratory Center where John W. had some friends and listened to their observations about cholera and its treatment.

From Bangkok, I went solo via Japan Air Lines to New Delhi and put up at the Imperial Hotel, strictly straight out of Kipling. My impressions of India were that it was squalid, dirty, poor, run-down, and broken down, both in buildings and in the mass of peoples. I figured from my short stay that our next war would probably be in India because (1) it was far away from the U.S. and (2) it was dirty, poor, stinking, and hot.

The one highlight of New Delhi and India was, of course, the *Taj*. The morning we were to go, I got up too late and missed the train to Agra. The hotel people helped me hire a Sikh driver with a car, and we took off! He spoke practically no English. As we left New Delhi, I didn't know whether I'd ever get back! He was the wildest driver! We almost hit three cars getting out of the hotel driveway as he scratched off. The wide city streets narrowed to four-lane highways to two-lane highways and finally to a narrow, twisting road. What with the cows, goats, camels, cars, trucks, people, small villages, and the road winding narrowly along, everyone, including the animals, seemed to play chicken out! Well, it was a hairy ride! I had been amazed to get out of Vietnam without getting zapped, and now I wondered whether I'd make it out of India! It was hot and dusty, and we covered the 125 miles to Agra in three hours flat. The land was flat, and looked like "Nam" except the smell in India was horses and cattle, a barnyard smell, rather than foul sewage. I was surprised at the large number of camels. We "did the Taj Mahal and Agra Fort." It was as beautiful and inspiring, as Richard Halliburton had convinced me years ago in the books and dreams of my childhood.

Everywhere someone wanted to sell you something, and the beggars, professional, amateur, real, or faked, were everywhere.

I left India feeling that, as a country, it was as bad as Vietnam, "therefore a good place for America to get involved in a war! Maybe only Afghanistan or Persia could be worse!"

After India, I traveled on KLM DC-8 to Athens with short stops in Karachi, Kuwait, and Beirut. (The brown-faced, bearded people looked meanly from their burnouses and flowing robes, and one felt uneasy among them.)

The customs in Athens opened my Coca-Cola tin suitcase. Everywhere it seemed to be eyed with suspicion or wonder. However, the weather was cooler and in spite of another kind of money to learn and worry with, the city was a perfect delight. I ran into Sam the Red Baron and he and I toured around together. I stayed at one of the most delightful, charming, small hotels I have ever visited in many years of traveling. It was frequented by the most gracious and pleasant English people, teachers, scholars, artists, etc., on vacation. We did all the usual, expected tourist things and with the Parthenon and Acropolis, I added to my growing list of Wonders of the Ancient World that I had visited.

Sam and I seemed to attract controversy. Weeks before in a Hong Kong discotheque, we had encountered young people tremendously antagonistic to American involvement in Vietnam (and for potentially helping!) and now in the National Museum, we quickly attracted a crowd of bearded, dirty, nasty, hippie, antiwar protesters, who for the most part, I was ashamed to find out, were Americans.

From Greece, I soloed via a BEA Comet to London where I was picked up by my sister-in-law and whisked at high speed in her Spitfire to Wales. England was as neat, pretty, charming, old, and well-kept as one had always read about. However, the English spring was late in arriving, and the weather was cold and rainy. I damn near froze to death for three days, as I had only short-sleeved shirts and tropical trousers—and very little of that. I'd given away my stuff in Vietnam and India, figuring I didn't need to impress anyone with my travel wardrobe. However, Sunny and her three charming and pretty girls kept me busy seeing the sights, and I soon was anxious to push along to the States and home.

The final journey from Heathrow via Pan Am to Kennedy was seven hours of misery. I had made it that far around the world, but I knew sooner or later my luck would run out! Sure enough, on this last leg, my boon seat companions were a couple of crying, squirming, climbing kids! I caught the late-afternoon Super Constellation shuttle to Washington and from there sat in a crowded Piedmont F-27, hedgehopping through Virginia and Carolina to home.

The night was dark and the air unsteady as we bumped along at low altitude, and I tried to talk to several people about where I'd been and what I'd been doing, but we couldn't really communicate, as I had my mind on coming back and they really couldn't comprehend the fantasy of the war I was expounding upon! The turbo-prop bounced in and whipped up to the terminal, and the pilot jockeyed the plane around, cutting the port engine, and many people got off. I was halfway back in the aisle and nervous.

As I walked from the stairway across the apron, I spotted them inside the glass window, and I quickened my walk to get through the door and into the waiting room.

There they were as I'd left them: Kay, Wes, Kathy, and Andy, all waiting; all waiting with love for me to come home. So glad to be home. For my safe deliverance and our reunion, I am grateful to God.

Home again.

On a fine day, in a warm wind, our heavenly guest
Will rise his brocade sail, cross
A thousand miles of waves,
Sailing where none of us can see.
This farewell cup in our hands we look down,
Already missing you. We will miss you more,
Soon, and you, we hope, will miss us, and our Southern land.
Tell the Emperor, please, exactly what we are!

To the Chinese Ambassador, at His Departure
—Ngo Chan Luc (19th Century)

EPILOGUE (1969)

Commander Joe O'M., *MC USNR*—reportedly transferred to Danang in June, but allegedly didn't like it, came home, and "got out." Called me in September (long distance) to let me know about it. Died 1970.

Lieutenant Commander Robert R., *MC USNR*—took over command, remained until end of year, and incidentally cleaned things up. Returned to U.S. Navy Hospital San Diego, passed orthopedic boards, and later in private practice.

Lieutenant Commander Anne W., *N.C. USNR*—transferred to Yokuska Naval Base Hospital in Japan.

Lieutenant Commander Anne W., *NCUSNR*—transferred to Yokuska Naval Base Hospital in Japan. Promoted to commander. Visited by Jerry H. early 1968 in Japan.

HC3—Dennis R.—Remained until end of year—went back to U.S.

Lieutenant JG Jerry H., *MSC USNR*—Transferred to 3rd Medical Battalion U.S. Marine Corps in I Corps at Phu Bai.

Katherine C., *RN USAID*—? went to Europe.

Beverly R., *RN USAID*—Transferred to Phu Vinh Hospital in Vinh Binh Province 1968—present in the '68 Tet outbreak.

Co Nguyet (Nurse)—Returned to Hue (?Lost in Tet '68), then to Danang to study anesthesia.

Co Thu (Nurse)—Returned to Can Tho U.S. Navy Dispensary.

Mr. Hoa—Interpreter—To schoolteaching position in primary school in Angiang Province.

Mr. Thank—Anesthetist—To Saigon for more training.

Mr. Day—Unknown.

Sister Clotilde—Unknown.

Dr. Tuan—Unknown.

Dr. Sam the Red Baron—Practicing general surgery in Asheville, N.C.

The Housekeepers—Bendix and his brother G.E. remained to take care of the doctors. Betty Crocker brought her husband Westinghouse to hospital in '68 with acute illness, type undetermined—very sick—she took him out against advice and he died.

The Hospital—In Tet '68 uprising, Rach Gia Hospital was mortared indiscriminately. The nurses' Bac Si House and the doctors' Bac Si House closed at night and all slept at hospital for security.

The Author—Of course, he went back. But then, that is another story!

SOURCES

The information referred to in the introductory portion was obtained from a nine-part series of articles "War Medicine in Vietnam" printed in the *Medical Tribune* (New York, N.Y.) in March and April 1966; the American Medical Association *NEWS* 19 September 1966; and the Sustaining Membership Lecture delivered to the Association of Military Surgeons of the United States seventy-fourth annual meeting, Washington, D.C., 21 November 1967, entitled "The A.I.D. Medical Mission in Vietnam" by Major General James W. Humphreys, Jr., U.S.A.F., M.C.

The narrative is a compilation and quotation of the following sources: "Bac Si My Vietnam 1967," The Diary of Wesley Grimes Byerly, M.D., a volunteer surgeon for the AMA-sponsored VPVN.

Hickory, North Carolina *Daily Record* "Medical Mission to Vietnam," by Dr. W. G. Byerly, 18 February 1967 and subsequent articles.

"The Practice of Wartime Civilian Surgery in South Vietnam," by Dr. W. Grimes Byerly, F.A.C.S. *The North Carolina Medical Journal*, October 1967, Vol. 28 No 10, pp. 409–416.

"Appendicitis in Wartime Civilian Surgical Practice in South Viet Nam" by W. Grimes Byerly, M.D.F.A.C.S., *The American Surgeon*, April 1968, Vol 34 No 4, pp. 268–269.

"Not Rare, Not Common," by M. Sgt. Donald F. Pratt, *Army* magazine, Jan. 1969, pp. 58–60.

4 Volumes of scrapbooks; 160 35-mm slides; and 1600 feet of 8-mm movie film.

Congressional Record, Proceeding of 90th Congress, First Session; Washington, D.C., Vol 113 #172, Wed. Oct 25, 1967, pp. 13977–80.

From the Vietnamese, Edited and translated by Burton Raffel. New York: October House, Inc., 1968.

GLOSSARY

AMA—American Medical Association

ARVN—Army Republic Vietnam—"*ARVINS*," applied loosely to all South Vietnamese Military

Bac Si My—American Doctor

BEQ—Bachelor Enlisted Quarters

BOQ—Bachelor Officer Quarters

"Charlie"—The Vietcong

CO—Commanding officer

CONUS—Continental United States

COVANS—Counterpart Vietnamese—American—slang for the American Military Advisors

Diuy—Rank of captain in Vietnamese army

Dong Y—Chinese Medical Man

Dust-Off—Slang for the U.S. Army medical evacuation helicopters

E.R., (D.)—Emergency Room (Department)

FAC—Forward Air Controller

G.P.—General Practitioner

Het Roi—All finished, done, dead.

I.V.—Intravenous

IV Corps—Four Corps—a political, military, geographic division of South Vietnam, composing several of the southernmost provinces.

MAAG—Military Advisory Assistance Team

MACV—Military Assistance Command-Vietnam

MEDCAP—Medical Civic Action Program (U.S. Army)

MID—Maternity-Infirmary-Dispensary (building and/or organization)

MILPHAP—Military Provincial Hospital Assistance Program (U.S. Army)

MPC—Military Payment Certificates—(Money)

Number One—The best

Number Ten—The worst, bad or no good.

OB—Obstetrics

OR—Operating Room (Suite)

P—Piasters (South Vietnamese monetary unit)

R & R—Rest and Recuperation (Military vacation)

RF-PF—Regional Forces-Popular Forces (Local militia-type troops)

Rough Puffs—Slang for above

RVN—Republic of Vietnam (South Vietnam)

Sin Loi—Excuse me; pardon

SOP—Standard Operating Procedure

SVN—South Vietnam

TOC—Tactical Operations Center

TSN—Ton Son Nhut (Saigon Airport)

USAF—United States Air Force

USAID—United States Agency for International Development (U.S. State Department)

USOM—United States Operations Mission (Local Overseas branches of USAID)

USN—United States Navy

VC—Vietcong

VPVN—Volunteer Physicians for Vietnam